STUDIO '3 E'

NEW EVERY MORNING

THE PRAYER-BOOK
OF THE
DAILY BROADCAST SERVICE

New every morning is the love
Our wakening and uprising prove;
Through sleep and darkness safely brought,
Restored to life, and power, and thought.

JOHN KEBLE

LONDON
THE BRITISH BROADCASTING
CORPORATION

REPRINTED 1939

CONTENTS

The following Abbreviations are used in the Forms of Service: A. & M. = *Hymns Ancient & Modern;* S.P. = *Songs of Praise;* M.P. = *Metrical Psalms;* Par. = *Paraphrase.*

FOREWORD

Among the many benefits bestowed upon the people of this country by the wonder of broadcasting, a special place must be given to the Daily Service. Day by day it unites multitudes of listeners in a fellowship of worship and prayer. People of every kind and class, especially workers in the home, the aged, and the sick, have found in it a source of strength, of solace, of tranquillity and trust. Their appreciation of the Service will be increased if they can have this book in their hands so that they may read as well as listen, and through the printed page refresh their memory of prayers, psalms, or hymns which, as they listened, touched their heart or quickened their spirit.

Moreover many who cannot listen, who are at work in the morning hour, will find this book a valuable guide and help to their own prayers.

I have read it carefully and it leaves on my mind the impression of just that temper of courage, cheerfulness, humble dependence upon God, and confident trust in him with which every day should begin, continue, and end. Some of its characteristics I venture specially to commend. It gives the rightful place, too often neglected, to reverent and adoring worship. It expresses the truth that prayer and supplication should always be accompanied by thanksgiving. Its intercessions have a singularly wide range and are themselves an education in the true scope of Christian prayer, and in the breadth of sympathy and remembrance which ought to mark the Christian mind. It gives the stimulus of variety both in the subjects and in the words of the prayers. There will be many, I expect, who will find, as I have done, new reason to value the old familiar Collects of the Book of

Common Prayer—their quietness, their reverent reserve, the beauty of their rhythm and language—when they come in the midst of other prayers longer, more eloquent, more fully expressive of the thoughts and needs of our modern life. Of course in such prayers phrases sometimes appear which may jar upon individual taste. Yet they have a wider range of thought and desire, they make a more varied appeal to the imagination, they express more intimately personal need and experience than is possible within the limits of the Collect.

I believe that this book, the result of much care, study, and thought, may meet a real need, and help all sorts and conditions of men to find 'new every morning' inspiration and guidance for their daily lives and help in that communion with God which is the highest activity of the human spirit.

COSMO CANTUAR:

LAMBETH PALACE
September, 1936.

INTRODUCTION

A WORD of introduction may be fitting on the publication of this book. As the science and art of broadcasting develop, so the demands of listeners and the possibilities of satisfying them expand and extend: the experiment of a few years' back is the commonplace of to-day. Among the early ventures of the B.B.C. was the daily religious Service. By now, difficult though it may be to estimate its full range and potency, this has become an established feature in the daily programmes; and requests have been received from an increasing number of listeners for a book of prayers fuller and more varied than any yet used. On one point all who made this request were agreed —that it would be wise to adhere to the form gradually evolved over many years' experience—and regular listeners at 10.15 a.m. will note that 'When Two or Three' (a book which has found its way into thousands of British homes, and on which for four years the Service has been based) was used as a model for its successor.

About eighteen months ago a small committee was appointed to co-operate with the B.B.C. Director of Religion in compiling a new book. The members of it were the Very Rev. Francis Underhill (Dean of Rochester), the Ven. Leslie Hunter (Archdeacon of Northumberland), the Rev. A. C. Craig (Chaplain of Glasgow University), the Rev. Hugh Martin (Editor of the Student Christian Movement Press), and the Rev. Edward Shillito (late Literary Secretary of the London Missionary Society); and for the invaluable service they have rendered the Corporation offers its cordial thanks. Many dozen books of devotion (ancient, medieval, and modern) have been consulted, and prayers from them reprinted: the oldest act of praise in this book has been used by Christians for

1,600 years; the newest prayer was written a few weeks ago. Acknowledgements to publishing firms and individuals will be found at the end of the book.

Each Service follows, roughly, the same plan: beginning with worship or praise or thanksgiving, passing to prayer for the wider needs of humanity, and ending with petitions for individual blessings. The title and text at the head of the Service explain its main content, and in the psalm, prayers, and hymns the theme is developed; but it should be understood that many of the intercessory prayers, without which no book of devotion would be complete, bear no special relation to the main subject of the Service, but have been inserted as appropriately as possible. Hymns relevant to Christian Festivals and other special occasions will also be sung in addition to those printed for regular use. The Bible texts at the head of each day's Service are taken from the Revised Version.

Two warnings should be added. First, it is not to be expected that each prayer in this book will make an equally strong and personal appeal to every listener; letters continuously received show how varied are the spiritual experiences and aspirations of those who join in the Service. A wide selection of prayers has, therefore, been included; and from these choice can be made, not only by the reader at the Service, but also by listeners who may find the book helpful in their private devotions. Secondly, there is no intention to use only the prayers here printed, or to use these only in their given context. Others will be offered, as need may arise; for the clamant and changing needs of the world and of our own country plead for a sanctified vigilance from all who worship in the fellowship of this Service.

September, 1936.   BROADCASTING HOUSE

OPENING SENTENCES

1. If any man will follow me, let him forsake himself and take up his cross and follow me. Whosoever shall endure unto the end, he shall be saved.

2. The hour cometh, and now it is, when true worshippers shall worship the Father in spirit and truth.

3. This is my commandment, that ye love together as I have loved you.

4. If any man love me, he will keep my word; and my Father will love him, and we will come unto him, and dwell with him.

5. I am the bread of life; he that cometh to me shall not hunger, and he that believeth on me shall never thirst.

6. I am the good shepherd; the good shepherd layeth down his life for the sheep. They shall become one flock, one shepherd.

7. I am the light of the world. He that followeth me shall not walk in darkness, but shall have the light of life.

8. Come unto me, all ye that labour and are heavy laden, and I will give you rest.

9. Why sleep ye? Rise and pray, lest ye enter into temptation.

Sentences 1 to 4 are taken from the First Prayer-book of Edward VI, and the text there used is here retained.

THE LORD'S PRAYER

OUR Father, which art in heaven, Hallowed be thy name; Thy kingdom come; Thy will be done; In earth as it is in heaven. Give us this day our daily bread. And forgive us our trespasses, As we forgive them that trespass against us. And lead us not into temptation; But deliver us from evil: For thine is the kingdom, The power, and the glory, For ever and ever. Amen.

A LISTENER'S PRAYER

ETERNAL God, who through thy Holy Spirit art everywhere present, calling us though we hear thee not, and abiding with us though we know thee not: we praise thee for the wonder of thy universe. We thank thee for the wisdom of scientists and the skill of craftsmen, whereby its secret forces become servants of the spirit of man. Grant that all who broadcast may use these forces in thy service, and that no word or sound may fall from them unfit for present needs or unworthy of their calling. And we ask that both they and all who hear may be led in the way of truth, love, and beauty to thee, the author and giver of all that is good; through Jesus Christ our Lord.

I

HOLY IS THE LORD

And one cried unto another, and said, Holy, holy, holy, is the Lord of hosts: the whole earth is full of his glory.

LET the name of God be hallowed. God is a Spirit: and they that worship him must worship in spirit and truth.

Thus saith the high and lofty one that inhabiteth eternity, whose name is Holy: I dwell in the high and holy place, with him also that is of a contrite and humble spirit, to revive the spirit of the humble, and to revive the heart of the contrite ones.

THEREFORE with angels and archangels, and with all the company of heaven, we laud and magnify thy glorious name, evermore praising thee and saying: Holy, holy, holy, Lord God of hosts, heaven and earth are full of thy glory. Glory be to thee, O Lord most high.

DELIVER us, O almighty God, when we draw nigh to thee, from coldness of heart and wanderings of mind: that with steadfast thought and kindled desire we may worship thee, in the faith and spirit of Jesus Christ our Lord.

OUR FATHER . . .

PSALM

63, 1–8. O God, thou art my God

99. The Lord is King, be the people never so unpatient

O LOVING Father, we thank thee for the care that has watched over us in the hours of darkness, and has given us once more this opportunity of uniting in prayer

B

and praise. To thee be the glory of all the good that we enjoy, for of thy hand do we receive it. To thee be the glory of all the good that we may think or do, for thy Spirit alone enables us. Give us grace, O God, to praise thee this day and evermore in our lives, studying in all things to please thee and to glorify thy name. Keep us pure and holy by the indwelling of thy Holy Spirit. Make us strong and of a good courage; may we remember that thou wilt never fail nor forsake us. Let neither the cares nor the business of the day disturb our trust in thee. We ask every blessing in the name and for the sake of Jesus Christ, our Lord and Saviour.

ALMIGHTY God, give to every country the spirit of human brotherhood: a new respect for man and for woman; new loyalty in service; new happiness in work and justice in reward; that in thee our homes may be restored and our cities re-built, and all the world may reflect thy light and thy love.

O GOD our Father, in whom all the families of the earth are blessed: we pray thee to regard with thy loving-kindness the homes of our country; that marriage may be held in due honour by the Church, by the State, and by society; and that husbands and wives may live faithfully together, in honour preferring one another. We pray that the members of every family may be rich in mutual understanding and forbearance, in courtesy and kindness, bearing one another's burdens, and so fulfilling the law of thy blessed Son, Jesus Christ our Lord.

SHEW us, O God, the way of patient industry: that, honouring and praising thee in the work of our hands, and learning the dignity of honest labour, we may be faithful in small and humble tasks, good comrades with our fellows, and brave to fight against all that may hinder fulness of life; through Jesus Christ our Lord.

Blessed Lord, who hast caused all Holy Scriptures to be written for our learning: grant that we may in such wise hear them, read, mark, learn, and inwardly digest them, that by patience, and comfort of thy holy Word, we may embrace and ever hold fast the blessed hope of everlasting life, which thou hast given us in our Saviour Jesus Christ.

O God, from whom all holy desires, all good counsels, and all just works do proceed: give unto thy servants that peace which the world cannot give; that both our hearts may be set to obey thy commandments, and also that by thee we being defended from the fear of our enemies may pass our time in rest and quietness; through the merits of Jesus Christ our Saviour.

We pray thee, O God, that thou wilt open our eyes to behold the heaven that lies about us: wherein they walk who, being born to the new life, serve thee with clearer vision and greater joy; for the sake of Jesus Christ our Lord.

We humbly beseech thee, O Father, mercifully to look upon our infirmities, and for the glory of thy name turn from us all those evils that we most righteously have deserved: and grant that in all our troubles we may put our whole trust and confidence in thy mercy, and evermore serve thee in holiness and pureness of living, to thy honour and glory; through our only mediator and advocate, Jesus Christ our Lord.

O CHRIST, our only Saviour: so dwell within us that, going forth with the light of hope in our eyes, thy word on our tongues, and thy love in our hearts, we may do the will of our heavenly Father, this day and evermore.

B LESSING, and glory, and wisdom, and thanksgiving, and honour, and power, and might, be unto our God for ever and ever. *Amen.*

HYMNS

A. & M.	S.P.	
161	460	Bright the vision that delighted
160	187	Holy, Holy, Holy! Lord God Almighty
548	556	Let all the world in every corner sing
	560	'Lift up your hearts!' We lift them, Lord, to thee
657	626	Praise to the Lord, the Almighty, the King of creation
706		Stand up and bless the Lord
M.P. 95, 1–6		O come, let us sing to the Lord

GLORY BE TO GOD ON HIGH

And in the morning, then ye shall see the glory of the Lord.

THOU, Lord, in the beginning hast laid the foundation of the earth: and the heavens are the work of thy hands. They shall perish, but thou shalt endure: they all shall wax old as doth a garment. They shall be changed: but thou art the same, and thy years shall not fail.

O GOD, who art from everlasting to everlasting, the creator and upholder of all things, the source of life and light: thy ways are not as our ways, nor thy thoughts as our thoughts; thy judgments are unsearchable, and thy ways past finding out.

Thou hast never left the world which thou hast made: day by day thou dost sustain it, bringing forth out of thy treasures things new and old. The seasons are thine with their changing beauty; the wealth of the earth is thine in its manifold splendour; all this thou hast given to man that he may use it and rejoice, seeing in it the bounty of thy love.

Throughout the ages thou hast led our race along the upward path, encouraging us by thy many gifts, schooling us by the discipline of suffering. Thy wisdom has been our guide; thy love has over-ruled our folly and our sin. Thou hast raised up great leaders in time of need; thou hast inspired explorers in every realm of knowledge; and in every age thou hast made known thy law, that in the fear of thee is the beginning of wisdom, and that without righteousness no nation can be great.

For thy wisdom, thy majesty, and thy beauty, we worship thee. Praise be to thy glorious name.

OUR FATHER . . .

PSALM

19, 1–9. The heavens declare the glory of God
96. O sing unto the Lord a new song

ALMIGHTY God, the fountain of all goodness, we humbly beseech thee to bless our Sovereign Lord the King, the Parliaments in all his dominions, and all who are set in authority under him: that they may order all things in wisdom, righteousness, and peace, to the honour of thy holy name, and the good of thy Church and people; through Jesus Christ our Lord.

ALMIGHTY and everlasting God, who dost govern all things in heaven and earth: mercifully hear the supplications of thy servants, and grant unto our country all things that are needful for its spiritual welfare. Strengthen and confirm the faithful; protect and guide the children; visit and relieve the sick and afflicted; turn and soften the wicked; rouse the careless; recover the fallen; restore the penitent. Remove all hindrances to the advancement of thy truth; and bring us all to be of one heart and mind in thy holy Church, to the honour and glory of thy blessed Son, Jesus Christ our Lord.

O GOD our Father, bless our friends and acquaintances, and all whom we shall meet this day: and grant that our intercourse in this world, whether for business or pleasure, may be hallowed by the presence of thy Son, Jesus Christ our Lord.

LOOK upon us, O Lord, and let all the darkness of our souls vanish before the light of thy glory. Fill us with holy love, and open to us the treasures of thy wisdom. All our desire is known unto thee; therefore perfect what thou hast begun, and what thy Spirit has awakened us to ask in prayer. We seek thy face; turn thy face unto us and shew us thy glory. Then shall our longing be satisfied, and our hearts be at peace.

ALMIGHTY God, we beseech thee to shew us thy glory. Help us to see thee in the universe around us, in the laws of nature, and in the longings of our souls. May we know more of thy fatherly goodness, through all that has been shewn to us by the experience of life and by the loving-kindness of men, and through all that our Lord revealed in his life and teaching. O loving Father, we pray thee to make us calm and strong in the faith that thou art always near, that thy love will never leave us nor forsake us, that thou art our refuge and underneath are thy everlasting arms. We praise and bless thee for all that gives strength and joy to our hearts, and for the ways in which we are held and guided on our daily path by the grace of our Lord Jesus Christ.

O GOD, who art the help and refuge of all thy children: from everlasting to everlasting thou art God. In our weakness thou art strength. In our darkness thou art light. In our sorrow thou art comfort and peace. We cannot number thy blessings; we cannot declare thy love. For all thy goodness we bless thee and praise thee. May we ever live as in thy presence, and love the things thou lovest, and serve thee with the service of our daily lives.

O ETERNAL Lord God, who holdest all souls in life: we beseech thee to shed forth upon thy whole Church, in paradise and on earth, the bright beams of thy light and heavenly comfort; and grant that, following the good example of those who have served thee here and are now at rest, we may at the last enter with them into the fulness of thine unending joy; through Jesus Christ our Lord.

To the only wise God, through Jesus Christ, be the glory for ever. *Amen.*

HYMNS

A. & M.	S.P.	
7	26	Christ, whose glory fills the skies
	499	Glad that I live am I
	558	Let the whole creation cry
169	581	My God, how wonderful thou art
522	595	O for a thousand tongues to sing
546	701	Ye holy angels bright
M.P. 145 (2), 1–6		O Lord, thou art my God and King

III

MAKER OF ALL THINGS

In the beginning God created the heaven and the earth. And God saw every thing that he had made, and, behold, it was very good.

And he that sitteth on the throne said, Behold, I make all things new.

O ETERNAL, immortal, invisible God, by whom all things are made, who through immeasurable time hast formed a world to be the home of mankind: we bless and praise thy name for the wonderful works which thou hast wrought through nature and through man. We praise thee for thy Holy Spirit ever working in the world and revealing new truth, and for the many blessings of this life: for the glorious beauty of the world of nature; for human love; for health and strength; for the joy of friendship; and for all the manifold interests of life. Above all we thank thee for the revelation of thyself to man through Jesus Christ, who for us men and for our salvation was made man, who suffered and was betrayed and crucified; yet death had no dominion over him, the author and giver of eternal life. Wherefore in praise and adoration, O Lord God almighty, we lift up our hearts unto thee.

Do thou of thy mercy, O God, keep us, who now worship thee, in holy fellowship with thee and with one another: cleanse us from all vain, wilful, and wandering thoughts; kindle our love and enlighten our understanding; that our prayers may come into the presence of thy divine majesty.

OUR FATHER . . .

PSALM

8. O Lord our Governor, how excellent is thy name in all the world

93. The Lord is King, and hath put on glorious apparel

O THOU who art the refuge of all who look to thee for succour: we commend to thy fatherly care all who are weary, faint-hearted, desperate, or incompetent, that in the hour of trial or failure, humiliation or unpopularity, thou wouldest uphold and strengthen them; we commend to thee the unemployed, the poor, the destitute; the homeless, the lonely, and the friendless; widows, orphans, and all who have been lately bereaved; the oppressed, ill-treated, wrongfully suspected, or punished; those tempted by others to sin, or persecuted for their faith; all who do not know their own needs, especially those who do not pray for themselves.

" O Lord Bless our pray

We pray for the sick and suffering, especially for cripples and invalids, the infirm and the deformed, the deaf, the dumb, and the blind; all who are in any adversity, that they may be given grace to avoid bitterness, self-pity, and despair, and that their sorrow may be turned into joy.

" O Lord hear our p

HEAR our humble prayer, O God, for all animals, especially for those in whose companionship and service we find joy and help. We entreat for them thy mercy and pity, and for those who deal with them we ask a heart of compassion, gentle hands, and kindly words. Make us all to be true friends of animals, and to share the blessing of the merciful; for the sake of thy Son, Jesus Christ our Lord. *" O Lord hear our prayers etc "*

Almighty and merciful God, who knowest the thoughts of our hearts: cleanse us, we beseech thee, from the stain of our past sins, and give us grace and power to put away all hurtful things; that we may be delivered from the bondage of sin, and may bring forth fruits worthy of repentance. Eternal goodness, deliver us from evil; eternal power, be thou our support; eternal wisdom, scatter the darkness of our ignorance; eternal pity, have mercy upon us: that with heart and mind and strength we may evermore seek thy face and, following in the footsteps of thy blessed Son, may obtain thy mercy, and enter into thy promised joy; through Jesus Christ, our only Saviour and Redeemer.

O God, who art the source of life and light and dost nourish and gladden all things in heaven and earth: we beseech thee mercifully to shine in our hearts; that the night and darkness of sin, and the mists of error on every side, being driven away by the brightness of thy light, we may all our life walk without stumbling, as in the day; and, being pure and clean from the works of darkness, may abound in all good works which thou hast prepared for us to walk in; through Jesus Christ our Lord.

Almighty and everlasting God: grant unto us purity of heart and strength of purpose, that no selfish passion may hinder us from knowing thy will, no weakness from doing it; but that in thy light we may see light, and in thy service find perfect freedom.

O GOD, who hast prepared for them that love thee such good things as pass man's understanding: pour into our hearts such love towards thee, that we loving thee in all things and above all things may obtain thy promises, which exceed all that we can desire; through Jesus Christ our Lord.

WORTHY art thou, our Lord and our God, to receive the glory and the honour and the power: for thou didst create all things, and because of thy will they were, and were created. *Amen.*

HYMNS

A. & M.	S.P.	
475	39	Behold us, Lord, a little space
	564	Lord of all being, throned afar
5		My Father, for another night
297	644	Songs of praise the angels sang
662	659	The spacious firmament on high
M.P. 148 (2)	657	The Lord of heaven confess

IV

THE KING IN HIS BEAUTY

Consider the lilies of the field, how they grow; they toil not, neither do they spin: yet I say unto you, that even Solomon in all his glory was not arrayed like one of these.

O ALL ye works of the Lord, bless ye the Lord : praise him and magnify him for ever.

O ye heavens, bless ye the Lord : O ye sun and moon, bless ye the Lord.

O ye showers and dew, bless ye the Lord : O ye winds of God, bless ye the Lord.

O let the earth bless the Lord : praise him and magnify him for ever.

O ye mountains and hills, bless ye the Lord : O all ye green things upon the earth, bless ye the Lord.

O all ye fowls of the air, bless ye the Lord : O all ye beasts and cattle, bless ye the Lord.

O ye children of men, bless ye the Lord : praise him and magnify him for ever.

O GOD, creator and Father, we praise thee for the marvel of beauty in which thou hast set our lives: for thy love, new every morning, shedding upon us the life-giving power of thy holiness. May we never accept as commonplace the mystery of creation. May the beauty of thy holiness flood our souls, washing away all that is mean and sordid; so that whatever work our hands shall find this day to do, we may do it to thy honour and glory.

OUR FATHER . . .

PSALM

104, 24–34. O Lord, how manifold are thy works
50, 1–15, 23. The Lord, even the most mighty God,
  hath spoken

O GOD, who once of old didst reveal thy Son Jesus
Christ to wise men studying the face of the heavens:
grant us to welcome the revelation of wisdom and science
through which in our own day thou dost make thy name
known among men. Reveal thyself again to men of
learning, that through their work the world may come
to know thee anew, and may offer new gifts and treasures
to the glory of thy name, who art evermore revealed in
thy Son, Jesus Christ our Lord.

O ALMIGHTY God, we pray thee to bless and prosper
the forces of the King: to succour, help, and comfort, all that are in danger, necessity, or tribulation,
(*especially* . . .); to preserve all that travel by air, or land,
or water; all women labouring of child, all sick persons,
and young children; to shew thy pity upon all prisoners
and captives; to defend and provide for the fatherless
children, and widows, and all that are desolate and
oppressed. We beseech thee, have mercy upon all men,
for the sake of him who bore our griefs and carried our
sorrows, Jesus Christ our Lord.

O GOD, who hast made all things, the flowers and trees
and the green grass, the sea, the sky, the stars, the
birds, and all living things: and hast made man in thine
own image, that he might know who is the creator of all
these things; open our eyes to see thee everywhere and
glorify thee in thy works; through Jesus Christ our Lord.

WE thank thee, O God of all the earth, for the beauty and strength of our land: for summer sun and winter frost, for bracing wind and quickening rain, for the changeful glory of sky and sea, of mountain, moor, and river. Enable us, by thy guidance, to serve the land we love, and ever look to thee as the author of all that we are and all that we have; for the sake of Jesus Christ our Lord.

O GOD, who hast wrought thy world with exceeding beauty: grant that we may shew forth thy praise by reverence towards all lovely things, and may study to preserve our countryside unspoilt. Give the nation wisdom to restrain those who in thoughtlessness or lust of gain would mar or destroy thy handiwork; we ask this for the sake of the generations to come, and for the glory of thy name.

ETERNAL God, by whose Spirit men are led into the way of blessedness: grant that the people of our land may feel after thee and find thee; and hasten the coming day when, sin and disease being subdued, our homes may be beautiful and our common life healthful and glad, to the hallowing of thy name.

MAKE us, O God, more worthy of thy many gifts. If we have been sullen and fretful, or mean and covetous, in the midst of them; if we have lived ugly lives in thy beautiful world; help us sincerely to repent. Forgive us; cleanse and save us. Make us, O heavenly Father, true followers day by day of him in whom the Word was made flesh and dwelt among men. So may we learn to look with pure and reverent eyes upon all thy creation, and glorify thee daily in our bodies and our spirits which are thine.

O GOD, whose never-failing providence ordereth all things both in heaven and earth: we humbly beseech thee to put away from us all hurtful things, and to give us those things which be profitable for us; through Jesus Christ our Lord.

BLESSED be the Lord God, who only doeth wondrous things: and blessed be his glorious name for ever; and let the whole earth be filled with his glory. *Amen.*

HYMNS

A. & M.	S.P.	
663	494	For the beauty of the earth
545	500	Glorious things of thee are spoken
	12	Let us, with a gladsome mind
	93	O worship the Lord in the beauty of holiness
378		Rejoice to-day with one accord
168	664	There is a book who runs may read

V

HE GIVETH LIBERALLY

He himself giveth to all life, and breath, and all things.

WITH humble thankfulness, O God, we acknowledge thy love to us thy children. We are not worthy of the least of thy mercies, but thou art the same, and thy love towards us cannot fail. Therefore, not trusting in our own righteousness but only in thy grace, we offer once again to thee the devotion of our hearts; through our Lord Jesus Christ.

LET us praise and thank God in gladness and humility for all great and simple joys:

For the gift of wonder and the joy of discovery, and for the constant newness of life:

For children and the joy of innocency; for the sanctities of family life, and for all that our friendships bring to us:

For the fruits of sympathy and sorrow; for the gift of humour and gaiety of heart; and for the joy of work attempted and achieved:

For the gifts of science and invention; for singers and all musicians; for poets and craftsmen; for those who work in form and colour to increase the beauty of life; for the consecration of art in the service of God; and for all things that help us to see the beauty of holiness:

For the grace of Christ in common people; their forbearance and generosity, their good temper, their courage, and their kindness; and for all humble lives of service.

OUR FATHER . . .

C

PSALM

146. Praise the Lord, O my soul; while I live will I praise the Lord

65. 1–8. Thou, O God, art praised in Sion

O GOD, the creator and preserver of all mankind, we humbly beseech thee for all sorts and conditions of men: that thou wouldest be pleased to make thy ways known unto them, thy saving health unto all nations. More especially we pray for the good estate of thy holy Church; that it may be so guided and governed by thy good Spirit, that all who profess and call themselves Christians may be led into the way of truth, and hold the faith in unity of spirit, in the bond of peace, and in righteousness of life. Finally, we commend to thy fatherly goodness all those who are any way afflicted or distressed in mind, body, or estate, (*especially* ...); that it may please thee to comfort and relieve them, according to their several necessities, giving them patience under their sufferings, and a happy issue out of all their afflictions. And this we beg for Jesus Christ his sake.

O ALMIGHTY God, look graciously upon our families and our homes. To parents give wisdom to direct those committed to their charge; to all give strength to fulfil thy will in the daily work to which thou shalt appoint them; that love and peace, with all other graces, may live and grow among us; through Jesus Christ our Lord.

ALMIGHTY God, who hast blessed the earth that it should be fruitful and bring forth abundantly whatever is needful for the life of man: give peace, we pray, in our borders, and satisfy our poor with bread. Prosper the labours of those who work on the land, and grant that we may gather the fruits of the earth in their season, and evermore rejoice in thy goodness.

WE ask for thy help, O Father, that in getting and spending we may not misuse thy gifts. Deliver us, in commerce and in sport, from the greed that seeks gain without labour, and the thrill of excitement without care for its cost to others. We pray that those in the grip of gambling habits may break free to become masters of themselves, and that we may be enabled to curb the power of those who exploit the weakness of their fellows. Prosper the efforts of all who seek to lift the drabness from men's daily lot, that all may find their joy in thee, and fulness of life in thy service; through Jesus Christ our Lord.

GIVE, O Lord, to all who till the ground wisdom to understand thy laws, and to co-operate with thy wise ordering of the world: and grant that the bountiful fruits of the earth may not be hoarded by the selfish or squandered by the foolish, but that all who work may share abundantly in the harvest of the soil; through Jesus Christ our Lord.

O GOD, who hast made the heavens and the earth and all that is good and lovely therein, and hast shewn us through Jesus, our Lord, that the secret of joy is a heart set free from selfish desires: help us to rejoice in the happiness of our neighbours, to find delight in simple things, and ever to be thankful for the richness of thy bounty.

ALMIGHTY God, who hast given unto us all things richly to enjoy: take from us the spirit of covetousness, and give us the spirit of service; that none may want, but each according to his need may share in thy bountiful liberality; for the sake of Jesus Christ our Lord.

St. Chrysostom Etc.

GRANT us, O Lord, to pass this day in gladness and peace, without stumbling and without stain: that we may reach the eventide victorious over all temptations, and may praise thee, the eternal God, who art blessed and dost govern all things, world without end.

O THOU, who art the sun of righteousness and the light eternal, giving gladness to all things: shine upon us both now and ever, that we may be glad and cheerful in thee.

THE grace of the Lord Jesus Christ, and the love of God, and the communion of the Holy Ghost, be with you all. *Amen.*

HYMNS

A. & M.	S.P.	
	535	Immortal, invisible, God only wise
4	31	New every morning is the love
	631	Rejoice, O land, in God thy might
290	677	Through all the changing scenes of life
517	694	When all thy mercies, O my God
	596 ⎫ Par. 2 ⎬	O God of Bethel, by whose hand

VI

HE CARETH FOR YOU

*O come let us worship and bow down; let us kneel before the
Lord our Maker: for he is our God, and we are the people of
his pasture, and the sheep of his hand.*

ALMIGHTY God, our heavenly Father, from whom
comes every good and perfect gift: we call to
remembrance thy loving-kindnesses and thy tender mercies
which have been ever of old; and we lift up our hearts
to thee in praise and thanksgiving.

We praise thee, O God, for all the gifts thou hast bestowed upon us and our race; for the life thou hast given
to us and the world in which we live:

For the order and constancy of nature; for the beauty and
bounty of the world; for day and night, summer and
winter, seed-time and harvest; for the varied gifts of love-
liness and use which every season brings:

For the comforts and joys of life; for our homes and our
friends; for the sympathy and good will of men; for the
help and counsel of those who are wiser and better than
ourselves:

For the heritage of our common life; for wise govern-
ment and good laws; for education and the benefits we
enjoy through science, literature, and art:

For the desire and power to help others; for every opportunity of serving our generation according to thy will,
and of manifesting the graciousness of Christ to men:

For thy grace bestowed upon us through Christ, in whom
we have pardon for sin and the power of a new life.

God of all grace and love; grant that, as we praise thee with our lips, so we may also praise thee in consecrated and faithful lives, and devote ourselves to thy service through the power of our Lord Jesus Christ.

OUR FATHER . . .

PSALM

34, 1–10. I will alway give thanks unto the Lord

29. Bring unto the Lord, O ye mighty, bring young rams unto the Lord

O GOD of our fathers, who art the protector of those who trust in thee: we commend to thy keeping the sailors and fishermen of our country, and all who earn their livelihood upon the great waters. May the fruits of their labour not be wasted through the sin or the folly of man. Enable them to face the perils of the sea and ride its storms with brave hearts and simple trust; and bring them to the haven where they would be.

O LORD Jesus Christ, who didst shew on this earth thy reverence and love for children: guard, we beseech thee, the children of our land, and remove all that may hinder them from being brought up in thy faith and love; who livest and reignest, God world without end.

O GOD our Father, bring to our remembrance all who are outcast in life, those who have not even one friend who cares for them, those who are bitter and angry with society, those condemned to long imprisonment. May all whom the love of their fellow-men cannot reach be found by thee; through him who came to seek and to save that which was lost, thy Son Jesus Christ our Lord.

Heavenly Father, who through thy Son Jesus Christ has taught us not to be anxious: we trust ourselves and our loved ones to thy tender care, knowing that underneath are thy everlasting arms, and praying thee to give us now and always that peace which the world cannot give, but which can be ours through Jesus Christ our Lord.

O Lord, our heavenly Father, be with us in our homes during the coming day. Make us to be loving and patient in our own families, forgiving others, as we remember how much we ourselves need to be forgiven. Keep us from all hastiness of temper, and all want of thoughtfulness for others in little things. Make us more ready to give than to receive; and grant that in our homes the holy law of love may reign, bringing to us a foretaste of thy Kingdom, where thy love shall be the everlasting joy of thy people for ever.

O God our Father, in whom we live and move and have our being, open our eyes that we may ever behold thy fatherly presence about us. Draw our hearts to thee with the power of thy love. Teach us to be anxious for nothing and, when we have done what thou hast given us to do, help us to leave the issue to thy wisdom. Take from us doubt and mistrust. Lift our thoughts up to thee in heaven, and make us to know that all things are possible to us through thy Son, our Saviour Jesus Christ.

LORD Jesus, who once didst lose the consciousness of thy Father's presence, living in the darkness, deprived of the sunshine of thy Father's face: teach us to be brave in times of depression and despair, when the clouds and the thick darkness are round about us; that so we may patiently endure the loss of heavenly comfort, and may know that at all times we are guarded by thy care, and kept in the safety of thy unfailing love.

THOU knowest, O God, how busy we must be this day: if we forget thee, do not thou forget us; for Christ's sake.

IN nothing be anxious; but in everything by prayer and supplication with thanksgiving let your requests be made known unto God. And the peace of God, which passeth all understanding, shall guard your hearts and your thoughts in Christ Jesus. *Amen.*

HYMNS

A. & M.	S.P.	
	438	All as God wills, who wisely heeds
373	503	God moves in a mysterious way
196	508	Guide me, O thou great Redeemer
276	604	O Lord, how happy should we be
	653	The God of love my shepherd is
	M.P. 23	The Lord's my shepherd, I'll not want

VII

*He restoreth my soul: he guideth me in the paths of righteous-
ness for his name's sake.*

G REAT art thou, O Lord, and greatly to be praised:
great is thy power, and thy wisdom is infinite. Thee
would we praise without ceasing. Thou callest us to
delight in thy praise, for thou hast made us for thyself,
and our hearts find no rest until they rest in thee.

A LMIGHTY God, we bow before thine infinite majesty
with lowly reverence: we remember that thou art
ever near thy children, waiting, with patience that wearies
not, to reveal thyself to those who will receive thee.
Come now into every heart, that this time of worship
may be to us the gate of heaven, and that in communion
with thee we may find strength and peace, and rise from
our prayer better fitted for our work. We ask this as
disciples of Jesus Christ our Lord.

W E give thee hearty thanks, O God, for the rest of
the past night and for the gift of a new day, with
all its opportunities of doing thy will. Grant that we may
so pass its hours in the perfect freedom of thy service,
that at eventide we may again give thanks unto thee;
through Jesus Christ our Lord.

OUR FATHER . . .

PSALM

25, 1–10. Unto thee, O Lord, will I lift up my soul; my
God, I have put my trust in thee

91, 1–11. Whoso dwelleth under the defence of the
most High

O GOD, who hast called our nation to a place of trust and responsibility throughout the world: we humbly thank thee for all the ways in which thou hast blessed and guided us unto this day. We confess before thee with shame all that has been unrighteous in our history, and all that even now makes us unworthy to be called a Christian people. Take from us, we pray thee, all pride and greed and injustice, and grant to us the spirit of unselfish service which alone can make us great; and may the love of Christ be so truly shewn forth through us, that his name shall be glorified among all nations; through the same Jesus Christ our Lord.

W E pray thee for those who bear authority in our towns and cities: that they may devote themselves to the common good, and that the skill and beauty of art and craft may be drawn into the service of our common life, for thy glory and the delight of man. Give them inspiration and courage, O God, to sweep away all mean streets and unworthy dwellings, and in all ways to forward the health and strength of thy people; through Jesus Christ our Lord.

O LORD, our heavenly Father, we commend to thy protecting care and compassion the men and women of our land now suffering distress and anxiety through lack of work: prosper, we pray thee, the counsels of those who are engaged in the ordering of our industrial life, that thy people may be set free from want and fear, and may be enabled to work in security and peace, for the happiness of our common life and the well-being of this realm.

O GOD, who hast shewn us through the life of thy Son the dignity of service: teach us to be courteous and considerate to all who serve us in shops and offices, on our journeys, and in our homes; that they may find joy and honour in their work, and may do it in praise of thee; through him who came to be the master and servant of us all, Jesus Christ our Lord.

GRANT unto us, almighty God, thy peace which passes understanding: that amid the temptations and troubles of life we may rest in thee, knowing that we are under thy care, governed by thy will, guarded by thy love; so that with a quiet heart we may face the storms of life, the cloud, and the thick darkness; ever rejoicing to know that the darkness and the light are both alike to thee. Guide, guard, and govern us even to the end, that none of us may fail to lay hold on the life eternal; through Jesus Christ our Lord.

O GOD, who hast taught us that we are most truly free when we find our wills in thine: help us to gain this liberty by continual surrender unto thee, that we may walk in the way which thou hast prepared for us, and in doing thy will may find our life; through Jesus Christ our Lord.

GOD almighty, eternal, righteous, and merciful: grant to us sinners to do for thy sake all that we know of thy will, and to will always what pleases thee; so that inwardly purified, enlightened, and kindled by the fire of the Holy Spirit, we may follow in the steps of thy Son, our Lord Jesus Christ.

O GOD, we beseech thee mercifully to receive the prayers of thy people which call upon thee: and grant that they may both perceive and know what things they ought to do, and also may have grace and power faithfully to fulfil the same; through Jesus Christ our Lord.

INTO thy hands, O Lord, we commit ourselves this day. Give to each one of us a watchful, humble, and diligent spirit, that we may seek in all things to know thy will; and when we know it may gladly perform it, to the honour and glory of thy name.

GRACE to you and peace from God the Father, and our Lord Jesus Christ. *Amen.*

HYMNS

A. & M.	S.P.	
6	24	At thy feet, O Christ, we lay
	487	Father, hear the prayer we offer
705	492	Fill thou my life, O Lord my God
695	501	God be in my head
165	598	O God, our help in ages past
	329	Turn back, O Man, forswear thy foolish ways

VIII

THE ETERNAL PURPOSE

God, having of old time spoken unto the fathers in the prophets by divers portions and in divers manners, hath at the end of these days spoken unto us in his Son.

BLESSED be thou, O God, who hast declared that it is thine eternal purpose to gather in one all things in Christ. Worthy art thou to receive honour and power and glory, for the great love wherewith thou hast loved all mankind, and hast delivered us from the powers of darkness, and brought us into the Kingdom of thy Son.

O GOD, who art and wast and art to come, before whose face the generations rise and pass away: age after age the living seek thee, and find that of thy faithfulness there is no end. Our fathers in their pilgrimage walked by thy guidance, and rested on thy compassion; still to their children be thou the cloud by day, and the fire by night. In our manifold temptations, thou alone knowest and art ever nigh; in sorrow, thy pity revives the fainting soul; in our prosperity and ease, it is thy Spirit only that can keep us from pride. O thou true source of peace and righteousness, take now the veil from every heart, and join us in one communion with thy prophets and saints who have trusted in thee and were not ashamed. Not for our worthiness, but of thy tender mercy, hear our prayer; for the sake of Jesus Christ thy Son our Lord.

ETERNAL God, the God of our fathers, the rock of our life, and the shield of our salvation: we give thanks unto thee and declare thy praise, for our lives which are committed to thy hand, and for our souls which are confided to thy care; for thy goodness which is displayed to us daily; for thy wonders and thy bounty which are at all times given to us. Thou art the most gracious, for thy mercies never fail; thou art the most compassionate, for thy loving-kindnesses never cease. Evermore do we hope in thee, O Lord our God.

OUR FATHER . . .

PSALM

90, 1–12. Lord, thou hast been our refuge

126. When the Lord turned again the captivity of Sion

O HEAVENLY Father, we pray thee to bless and protect thy servants who have gone forth to preach the gospel in distant lands: give them such success in their labours that thy way may be known upon earth, thy saving health among all nations. Hear and grant our prayer, O God, for the sake of Jesus Christ, our blessed Lord and Saviour.

O GOD, who hast sent thy Son Jesus Christ to be the great physician of our bodies: bless, we beseech thee, all whom thou hast called to share in thy work of giving health to men, and enable us to learn and obey thy laws; so that our spirits, minds, and bodies may be presented before thee without blemish, to the praise and glory of thy name; through the same thy Son Jesus Christ our Lord.

REMEMBER, O Lord, all who have wandered from thy ways, especially those who have brought trouble and misery upon themselves: take from them all blindness of mind and hardness of heart; bring them home to thee; give them hope and strength to begin again; and grant to us the love and the wisdom to help them; through Jesus Christ our Lord.

O GOD our heavenly Father, who providest for the bodily needs of thy children: enlighten the ignorance and forgive the sin whereby men have abused thy providence and squandered thy gifts. Inspire us to share more justly thy bounty, so that we may be better able to serve thee with glad and quiet minds; through Jesus Christ our Lord.

O GOD, who rulest the world from everlasting to everlasting: speak to our hearts when courage fails, and we faint for fear; when our love grows cold, and there is distress of nations upon the earth. Keep us resolute and steadfast in the things that cannot be shaken, abounding in hope and knowing that our labour is not in vain in thee. Restore our faith in thine eternal purpose; renew in us that love which never fails; and make us to lift up our eyes and to behold, beyond the things which are seen and temporal, the things which are unseen and eternal.

ALMIGHTY God, the Father of our Lord Jesus Christ: deliver us now from the vain things which have power over us, and enable us to rest our souls in thee and yield ourselves to the guidance of thy loving Spirit. Make us ready to offer thee the joy that is thy gift, and worship thee with glad and thankful hearts. In the light of thy perfection help us to see our shortcomings, and to repent of our faults; and grant, we beseech thee, that strengthened by our common worship we may serve thee and our fellow men more faithfully in our daily lives, and come at last to thine eternal Kingdom; through the same Jesus Christ our Lord.

UNTO him that is able to do exceeding abundantly above all that we ask or think, according to the power that worketh in us, be the glory in the Church and in Christ Jesus unto all generations for ever and ever. *Amen.*

HYMNS

A. & M.	S.P.	
	28	Father, we praise thee, now the night is over
735	300	God is working his purpose out as year succeeds to year
586	301	Lift up your heads, ye gates of brass
	602	O life that makest all things new
	312	These things shall be! A loftier race
	680	Thy Kingdom come! On bended knee

IX

AND WAS MADE MAN

Have this mind in you, which was also in Christ Jesus: who, being in the form of God, counted it not a prize to be on an equality with God, but emptied himself, taking the form of a servant, being made in the likeness of men.

Blessed be God, who sent his Son to live our human life: who as a father pities our weakness, giving help in time of need; in sorrow, comfort; in temptation, strength; and, in death, the sure and certain hope of life eternal. Blessed be God.

Glory be to God on high, and in earth peace, good will towards men. We praise thee, we bless thee, we worship thee, we glorify thee, we give thanks to thee for thy great glory, O Lord God, heavenly King, God the Father Almighty.

O Lord, the only-begotten Son, Jesu Christ; O Lord God, Lamb of God, Son of the Father, that takest away the sins of the world, have mercy upon us. Thou that takest away the sins of the world, have mercy upon us. Thou that takest away the sins of the world, receive our prayer. Thou that sittest at the right hand of God the Father, have mercy upon us.

For thou only art holy; thou only art the Lord; thou only, O Christ, with the Holy Ghost, art most high in the glory of God the Father.

OUR FATHER . . .

D

PSALM

98.   O sing unto the Lord a new song

111.   I will give thanks unto the Lord with my whole heart

WE bring before thee, O Lord, the troubles and perils of people and nations: the sighing of prisoners and captives; the sorrows of the bereaved; the necessities of strangers; the helplessness of the weak; the despondency of the weary; the failing powers of the aged. O Lord, draw near to each, and teach them, in their hour of need, to draw near to thee.

REMEMBER, Lord, the place in which we dwell, and every town and village, and the faithful that live in them. Remember those that travel, those that are sick or afflicted. Remember those that do good deeds and forget not the poor. Send forth on us all the riches of thy compassion, and grant us with one mouth and one heart to glorify thy name.

WE pray thee, O Father, to look in mercy on all women who are facing the pain and peril of childbirth. Grant to them courage, and patience, and the reward of a great joy; for the sake of him who sanctified all human motherhood by his birth at Bethlehem, Jesus Christ our Lord.

O FATHER of mercies, and God of all comfort, who hast made man's body to be a temple of the Holy Spirit: sanctify, we pray thee, all those whom thou hast called to study and practise the art of healing the sick, and the prevention of disease and pain. Strengthen them with thy life-giving Spirit, that by their sacred ministry the health of thy people may be established; through thy Son, Jesus Christ our Lord.

O GOD, the King of righteousness, lead us, we pray thee, in ways of justice and peace: inspire us to break down all tyranny and oppression, to gain for every man his due reward, and from every man his due service; that each may live for all and all may care for each, in Jesus Christ our Lord.

O GOD our Father, who didst so love the world as to give thine only-begotten Son: grant us both the desire and the will to love thee in return. Help us this day, amid our manifold interests and duties, at all times to remember thee and, alike by what we do and what we are, to render thee faithful and loving service. Deliver us from indolence and weakness; teach us to look away from ourselves to the hopes and needs of others; and grant us power so to use the gifts thou hast bestowed on us as to brighten and ennoble the life of the world; through Jesus Christ our Lord.

O LORD Jesus, who didst carry through the work which thy Father gave thee to do, even unto the end, grant us not to be weary in well doing: teach us to endure, to pray and not to faint, to work and not to fall into idleness, cynicism, or despair; to drink without fear of the cup which our heavenly Father gives us to drink, waiting in patience for the reward of knowing thee, and of being satisfied with thy presence for evermore.

Almighty God, who hast given to thy people the true bread which comes down from heaven, even thy Son Jesus Christ: may our souls be so fed by him who gives health unto the world, that we may abide in him and he in us, and thy Church may be filled with the power of his deathless life.

Almighty God, who didst wonderfully create man in thine own image, and didst yet more wonderfully restore him: grant, we beseech thee, that as thy Son our Lord Jesus Christ was made in the likeness of men, so we may be made partakers of the divine nature; through the same thy Son, who with thee and the Holy Ghost liveth and reigneth, one God, world without end.

The Lord bless you, and keep you: the Lord make his face to shine upon you, and be gracious unto you: the Lord lift up his countenance upon you, and give you peace. *Amen.*

HYMNS

A. & M.	S.P.	
	72	Behold the great creator makes
164		Father of heaven, whose love profound
53	62	Hark the glad sound! The Saviour comes
642	79	O little town of Bethlehem
	682	To Mercy, Pity, Peace, and Love
	96 } Par. 19 }	The race that long in darkness pined

X

I WILL HELP THEE

For we have not a high priest that cannot be touched with the feeling of our infirmities; but one that hath been in all points tempted like as we are, yet without sin. Let us therefore draw near with boldness unto the throne of grace, that we may receive mercy, and may find grace to help us in time of need.

AND it shall come to pass that before they call I will answer: and while they are yet speaking I will hear.

WORTHY art thou, O Lord of heaven and earth, to receive glory, and honour, and power: for thou hast created all things, and for thy pleasure they were, and were created. Thou hast made the heavens with all their host, the earth and all things that are therein; thou preservest them all, and the host of heaven praiseth thee. Glory be to thee, O Lord God Almighty, for creating man after thine own image, and making so great a variety of creatures to minister to his use. But, above all, glory be to thee for giving thine only Son to die for our sins, and for all the spiritual blessings he has won for us. For whatever sin we have escaped, for whatever good we have done or thought, for the help of thy grace, and for our hopes of heaven; glory be to thee, O God.

OUR FATHER . . .

PSALM

130. Out of the deep have I called unto thee, O Lord

4. Hear me when I call, O God of my righteousness

WE pray to thee, O God our heavenly Father, for all seafarers and for those who serve their needs: for the officers and men of the Royal Navy and the Mercantile Marine; for the keepers of lighthouses and the pilots of our ports; for those who man life-boats and guard our coasts; for the men of the fishing-fleets and those who carry out the services of docks and harbours; and for all guilds and societies which care for the well-being of sailors and their families. Bless them according to their several necessities, and keep them in all dangers and temptations.

O GOD, the only source of truth, direct with thy wisdom the work of education in all lands. Give to teachers the spirit of understanding, and the wisdom to unite old traditions with new knowledge. Especially we pray for those who are disheartened by the conditions of their work and are losing their courage and vocation, that thou wilt refresh and sustain them. Above all give them that grace and beauty of life without which knowledge is vain, and that faith in thee which makes men humble seekers of truth throughout their days. We ask it as disciples of Jesus Christ.

O GOD our Father, in whom we are all one family, united by thy Spirit in the one body of thy Son, Jesus Christ our Lord: we remember before thee our friends who are absent from us to-day; the boys and girls at school; the men and women abroad in distant parts of the Empire, especially the homesick and the friendless; and all good and faithful people gone before us, who are now at rest.

O GOD, who art the author of peace and lover of concord, in knowledge of whom standeth our eternal
life, whose service is perfect freedom: defend us thy
humble servants in all assaults of our enemies, that we
surely trusting in thy defence may not fear the power of any
adversaries; through the might of Jesus Christ our Lord.

ALMIGHTY God, give us grace to contend always for
what is true and right: and to be ready, if need be, to
suffer for it. Give us not over to any death of the soul,
but lift us into newness of life, and let us glorify and
enjoy thee for ever.

O GOD, who knowest us to be set in the midst of so many
and great dangers, that by reason of the frailty of
our nature we cannot always stand upright: grant to us
such strength and protection as may support us in all
dangers and carry us through all temptations; through
Jesus Christ our Lord.

GRANT, we beseech thee, merciful God, to thy faithful
people pardon and peace: that they may be cleansed
from all their sins, and serve thee with a quiet mind;
through Jesus Christ our Lord.

O GOD our Father, whose secret is with them that fear
thee: let not the darkness of our folly and selfishness
come any more between us and thee; through Jesus Christ
our Lord.

O GOD, the King eternal, who dividest the day from
the darkness, and turnest the shadow of death into
the morning: drive far off from us all wrong desires,

incline our hearts to keep thy law, and guide our feet into the way of peace; that, having done thy will with cheerfulness while it is day, we may when the night comes rejoice to give thee thanks.

O LORD, support us all the day long of this troublous life: until the shades lengthen, and the evening comes, and the busy world is hushed, the fever of life is over, and our work done. Then, Lord, in thy mercy, grant us safe lodging, a holy rest, and peace at the last; through Jesus Christ our Lord.

U NTO him that is able to guard you from stumbling, and to set you before the presence of his glory without blemish in exceeding joy, to the only God our Saviour, through Jesus Christ our Lord, be glory, majesty, dominion, and power, before all time, and now, and for evermore. *Amen.*

HYMNS

A. & M.	S.P.	
282	100	Be thou my guardian and my guide
	330	Father all-seeing, friend of all creation
	488	Father in Heaven, who lovest all
257	529	I heard the voice of Jesus say
281	555	Lead us, heavenly Father, lead us
	583	My God, my Father, make me strong
M.P. 19, 7–11		God's law is perfect, and converts

XI

THE IMAGE OF GOD

No man hath seen God at any time; the only begotten Son, which is in the bosom of the Father, he hath declared him.

To give the light of the knowledge of the glory of God in the face of Jesus Christ.

PRAISE be to thee, O God, who through thy Son Jesus Christ hast revealed thyself to the world. Praise be to thee, O God, that the light of the gospel of the glory of Christ, who is the image of God, has shined upon them that believe. Blessed be the Lord God of Israel, for he hath visited and redeemed his people: to give light to them that sit in darkness, and in the shadow of death, and to guide our feet into the way of peace.

ALMIGHTY God, who art our life, our health, and our joy: we praise and thank thee for thy gifts to us and to all men. We thank thee for life, with its blessings of health and strength; for its affections and sympathies, and all its ways of doing good; for whatever measure thou hast taught us of thy truth; for leading us through Jesus Christ nearer to thee; and for giving us a hope full of immortality. And, we beseech thee, multiply thy grace upon us, that no ignorance or sin may turn thy blessings into curses; but give us such a lively sense of thy goodness, that we may ever devote ourselves to thy will and service, and through thy mercy attain to the joy of everlasting life.

OUR FATHER . . .

PSALM

103, 1–13. Praise the Lord, O my soul

119, 137–144. Righteous art thou, O Lord

WE beseech thee, almighty Father, to be our help and succour. Save those who are in tribulation; have mercy on the lonely; lift up the fallen; show thyself to the needy; heal the ungodly; bring home the wanderers; feed the hungry; raise up the weak; comfort the faint-hearted. Let the whole world know that thou art God alone, that Jesus Christ is thy Son, and that we are thy people and the sheep of thy pasture.

O GOD, who hast created and hallowed all human affections, and dost raise our frail nature by thy grace: send thy blessing, we pray thee, upon all who are in love; preserve them from the blindness of unenlightened ignorance and from the weakness of ungoverned passion; that, through the sanctifying strength of thy Holy Spirit, they may find their true happiness and affection for one another in an ever-deepening devotion to thee; through Jesus Christ our Lord.

HEAVENLY Father, from whom all fatherhood in heaven and earth is named: bless, we beseech thee, all children, and give to their parents, and to all in whose charge they may be, thy Spirit of wisdom and love; so that the home in which they grow up may be to them an image of thy Kingdom, and the care of their parents a likeness of thy love.

ETERNAL God, who committest to us the solemn trust of life: since we know not what a day may bring forth, but only that the hour for serving thee is always present, may we wake to the instant claims of thy holy will, not waiting for to-morrow, but yielding to-day. Consecrate with thy presence the way our feet may go, that the humblest work may shine, and the roughest place be made plain. Lift us above unrighteous anger and mistrust into faith and hope and love, by simple reliance on thy sure will. In all things draw us to the mind of Christ, that thy lost image may be traced again; to the glory of thy great name.

O GOD, who hast commanded us to be perfect, as thou our Father in heaven art perfect: plant in our hearts, we pray thee, a continual desire to obey thy holy will. Teach us day by day what thou wouldest have us do, and give us grace to do it. May we never from love of ease decline the path which thou dost appoint, nor for fear of shame turn away from it; for the sake of Jesus Christ our Lord.

O THOU who art the light of the minds that know thee, the life of the souls that love thee, and the strength of the wills that serve thee: help us so to know thee that we may truly love thee; so to love thee that we may fully serve thee, whom to serve is perfect freedom.

O HOLY and ever-blessed God: teach us, we beseech thee, to love one another, to exercise forbearance and forgiveness towards our enemies, to recompense no man evil for evil, but to be merciful even as thou, our Father in heaven, art merciful; that so we may continually follow after thee in all our doings, and be more and more conformed to thine image and likeness; and this we ask through Jesus Christ our Lord.

O HOLY Spirit, renew us day by day and fashion us after the image of God: let all bitterness be put away from us, all wrath, and anger, and clamour, and evil speaking, with all malice; may we be kind one to another, tender-hearted, forgiving one another, even as God also in Christ forgave us.

THE God of hope fill you with all joy and peace in believing, that ye may abound in hope, in the power of the Holy Ghost. *Amen.*

HYMNS

A. & M.	S.P.	
	536	Immortal love, for ever full
	552	Judge eternal, throned in splendour
520	573	Love divine, all loves excelling
298	623	Praise, my soul, the King of heaven
292	624	Praise the Lord! Ye heavens, adore him
197	654	The King of love my shepherd is

XII

THE KINGDOM OF GOD IS AT HAND

There followed great voices in heaven, and they said, The kingdom of the world is become the kingdom of our Lord, and of his Christ: and he shall reign for ever and ever.

THOU art worthy, O God, to receive honour, and glory, and blessing.

Blessed be thy glorious name, that in every place the faith of Christ is spread abroad: all glory be to thee, O Lord.

For thy good soldiers in every age striving lawfully, enduring unto the end; for all the signs of thy presence, for all the marks of thy Cross: we bless and praise thy glorious name.

For the light of thy everlasting gospel, sent to every nation, and kindred, and people, shining so long among ourselves: all glory be to thee, O Lord.

For thy word of promise that they that be wise shall shine as the brightness of the firmament, and they that turn many to righteousness as the stars for ever and ever: all glory be to thee, O Lord.

O KING of men and master of our lives, entering into glory by thy Cross, to whom all authority is given both in heaven and upon earth: come, Christ, enter into thy Kingdom; subdue the world by the power of thy love, and be known and adored to all ends of the earth.

OUR FATHER . . .

PSALM

145, I–I3. I will magnify thee, O God, my King

MAGNIFICAT.   My soul doth magnify the Lord

O GOD, our King, who hast called us through Jesus Christ to be kings and priests unto thee: teach us to bear one another's burdens and the burdens of the commonwealth. Open the eyes of us all to see the woes of our land, the despair in the lives of many of our fellow-citizens, the deep and shameful wrongs that cry to be put right. Give to us also a vision of our land as thou wouldest have it be, and as thou alone canst remake it. Take us, we humbly beseech thee, to be thy servants, giving us no rest or discharge until thou hast wrought this work of pity, that generations yet unborn may praise thy name.

O GOD the Father of all, who hast created men to glorify thee in the freedom of thy service: pour thy blessing upon all engaged in professions, in commerce, in agriculture, in crafts, and in all forms of manual labour; especially upon workers in the mines and in dangerous trades. Grant them skill and progress in knowledge, honesty and faithfulness in labour, thy protection in danger. May there ever be goodwill and Christian action between ranks and classes, employers and employed, masters and servants, rich and poor; and may all men know their unity in the great family which is thine; through Jesus Christ our Lord.

T EACH us, O God, to see every question of foreign policy in the light of our faith: that we may check in ourselves and in others every temper which makes for war, all ungenerous judgments, all promptings of self-assertion, all presumptuous claims; and, being ever ready to recognize the needs and aspirations of other peoples, we may, with patience, do whatever in us lies to remove suspicions and misunderstandings; and to honour all men in Jesus Christ our Lord.

G RACIOUS Father, whose Son knew the saving and contriving of the frugal home, where the lost coin must be searched for because it was precious: be with us in our planning to make small means go far, and keep us through the coming hours by thy grace; so that, when our children and our men come home at end of day, we may meet happily and at peace in the shelter of thy care; through Jesus Christ our Lord.

O LORD, who hast set before us a great hope that thy Kingdom shall come on earth, and hast taught us to pray for its coming: make us ever ready to thank thee for the signs of its dawning, and to pray and work for the perfect day when thy will shall be done, on earth as it is in heaven.

O GOD, thou lover of men's lives, be merciful to all who through the fault of others or their own are unsuccessful or inefficient: give courage to the doubting and the despairing; have pity on all who are without work, and stir the wills and imaginations of those who are trying to help them; for Jesus Christ's sake.

O LORD, we humbly beseech thee, blot out our past transgressions, heal the evils of our negligences and ignorances, and make us amend our mistakes and misunderstandings: lift up our hearts to new love, new energy and devotion, that we may be released from the grief and shame of past unfaithfulness, and may go forth in thy strength to persevere through success and failure, through good report and evil report, even to the end. And in all time of our tribulation, in all time of our wealth, save us and help us, we humbly beseech thee, O Lord.

GRANT to us, Lord, we pray thee, day by day the joy of true living: that we who seek thy service may find thy peace.

ALL blessing and thanksgiving be to God our Father, whose good pleasure it is to give us the kingdom. *Amen.*

HYMNS

A. & M.	S.P.	
	468	City of God, how broad and far
220	545	Jesus shall reign where'er the sun
665	553	King of glory, King of peace
	307	O brother man, fold to thy heart thy brother
	635	Rise up, O men of God!
	658	The Lord will come and not be slow
Par. 20, 1–5		How glorious Sion's courts appear

XIII

CHILDREN OF OUR FATHER

Behold what manner of love the Father hath bestowed upon us, that we should be called children of God.

BLESSED be the God and Father of our Lord Jesus Christ, the Father of mercies and God of all comfort, who comforteth us in all our tribulation. O praise our God, ye peoples, and make the voice of his praise to be heard: who holdeth our soul in life and suffereth not our feet to slip; who forgiveth all our sin and healeth all our infirmities; who saveth man from destruction and crowneth him with mercy and loving-kindness. Blessed be the name of the Lord: from this time forth for evermore.

O ALMIGHTY God, we praise thee, we worship thee, we give thanks to thee, the Father everlasting: Father of our Lord Jesus Christ, and our Father. For all the things that make our passing days beautiful, we devoutly thank thee: for the heavens above and the earth beneath, and for the life which goes forth evermore from thee; for labour and rest, for joy and sorrow; for the mercies that make us glad; and for the trials that warn us to renew our trust and to possess our souls in patience. We bless thee for thy redeeming love revealed to us in the life and the Cross of thy beloved Son, and for the grace by which we are his disciples. We bless thee for the manifold gifts of thy Spirit; for the fellowship of all Christian people; for this world of rich opportunities; and for the hopes and promises of the world that is to come.

OUR FATHER . . .

E

PSALM

112, 1–7. Blessed is the man that feareth the Lord

82. God standeth in the congregation of princes

O GOD, our heavenly Father, high and mighty, King of kings, Lord of lords, the only ruler of princes, who dost from thy throne behold all the dwellers upon earth: most heartily we beseech thee with thy favour to behold our most gracious Sovereign Lord, King George: and so replenish him with the grace of thy Holy Spirit, that he may alway incline to thy will, and walk in thy way. Endue him plenteously with heavenly gifts; grant him in health and wealth long to live; strengthen him that he may vanquish and overcome all his enemies; and finally, after this life, he may attain everlasting joy and felicity; through Jesus Christ our Lord.

ALMIGHTY God, the fountain of all goodness, we humbly beseech thee to bless our gracious Queen Elizabeth, Mary the Queen Mother, the Princess Elizabeth, and all the Royal Family: endue them with thy Holy Spirit; enrich them with thy heavenly grace; prosper them with all happiness; and bring them to thine everlasting King- dom; through Jesus Christ our Lord.

O GOD, almighty Father, King of kings and Lord of lords: grant that the hearts and minds of all who go forth as leaders among us, the statesmen, the judges, the men of learning, and the men of wealth, may be so filled with the love of thy laws, and of that which is righteous and life-giving, that they may be worthy stewards of thy good and perfect gifts; through Jesus Christ our Lord.

O GOD of peace, our Father, we come to thee for refuge from the noise and hurry of the world, and the oppression of selfish thoughts and fears. Deliver us from the sin which hides thee from us, and give us thy peace. Grant that the Spirit who dwelt in thy Son without measure may also dwell in us, so that we may worship thee in humility and gladness, and go forth again with hearts made cheerful and strong by the knowledge of thy love.

O ALMIGHTY God, who alone canst order the unruly wills and affections of sinful men: grant unto thy people that they may love the thing which thou commandest, and desire that which thou dost promise; that so, among the sundry and manifold changes of the world, our hearts may surely there be fixed where true joys are to be found; through Jesus Christ our Lord.

GRANT, O God, we beseech thee, that the course of this world may be so peaceably ordered by thy governance, that thy Church may joyfully serve thee in all godly quietness; through Jesus Christ our Lord.

ALMIGHTY and everlasting Father, who art ever present with us in all the duties of our life at home: grant that we may know thee to be the defender of our households and the master of our dwellings; through Jesus Christ our Lord.

O LORD and Saviour, who by thy words and thy life hast taught us how true men should live: we would take thy yoke upon us and learn of thee. Grant unto us now and at all times thy spirit of kindliness and goodwill;

inspire in our hearts thy love for God and man; and help us all our days to follow humbly in thy footsteps.

To thine eternal faithfulness and love we commend ourselves and all who are dear to us. And unto thee, O God our Father, be all glory and praise from the whole Church of Jesus Christ, world without end.

May our Lord Jesus Christ himself, and God our Father which loved us and gave us eternal comfort and good hope through grace, comfort your hearts and stablish them in every good work and word. *Amen.*

HYMNS

A. & M.	S.P.	
3	25$^{(1)}$	Awake, my soul, and with the sun
	481	Dear Lord and Father of mankind
8		Forth in thy name, O Lord, I go
	285	From thee all skill and science flow
403	217	Jesus calls us! O'er the tumult
	540	Jesus, good above all other

XIV

HE HEALED THEM

And Jesus went about preaching the gospel of the kingdom, and healing all manner of disease and all manner of sickness among the people.

ALL glory, thanks, and praise be to thee, O Lord our God and Saviour, for all who have made life happier and smoother for others: for those who have inspired us by their example and encouraged us by their words; for those who take up their cross and follow thee; for those who tread the way of sorrow in the calm of faith; for those who battle for the right in thy strength; for those who bear pain with grace and patience; for those who by thy heavenly wisdom are enabled to teach the way of true life; for those who love others unselfishly in thee.

ENLARGE our souls, O God, with a divine charity, that we may hope all things and endure all things: and may become messengers of thy healing mercy to the grievances and infirmities of men; through Jesus Christ our Lord.

OUR FATHER . . .

PSALM

23. The Lord is my shepherd

121. I will lift up mine eyes unto the hills

FATHER, let thy healing hand be laid upon this world which thou hast created and which thou lovest. Shew us where we have gone wrong, through avarice, or selfishness, or lazy acquiescence in wrong-doing. Stir up,

O Lord, our wills and kindle our imaginations, that we may find the way to a just and ordered society, where all may work and all may gain a due reward, and thy people may serve thee and one another in peace and goodwill, in the spirit of thy Son, Jesus Christ our Lord.

O GOD our Father, we pray for all on whom is laid the cross of suffering: the sick in body and the weak in mind; all who have lost relations or friends; all who are troubled by the suffering or sin of those they love; all who have met with worldly loss; that in the cloudy and dark day they may find assurance and peace in thee. We pray for all who are absorbed in their own grief, that they may be raised to share the sorrows of their brethren, and know the secret and blessed fellowship of the Cross; for all who are lonely and sad in the midst of others' joy, that they may know thee as their friend and comforter. Remember, O Lord, the aged and infirm, those who feel that their life's work is done and can no longer lend a helping hand where once they did; all who are passing through the valley of shadows, that they may know that the risen Christ is with them, and that there is light at evening time.

ALMIGHTY God, whose blessed Son Jesus Christ went about doing good, and healing all manner of disease among the people: continue, we beseech thee, his gracious work among us, especially in all hospitals, infirmaries, and nursing homes. Cheer, heal, and sanctify the sick; grant to all physicians, surgeons, and nurses, both wisdom and skill, sympathy and patience; and send thy blessing on all who labour to prevent suffering and to forward thy purpose of love.

O GOD, who art the author of light, and with whom is no darkness at all: we thank thee for the good gift of sight which thou hast bestowed upon us, and we pray thee to fill us with thine own compassion for those who have it not. Direct and prosper the efforts that are made for their welfare. Reveal to them by thy Spirit the things that eye has not seen; and comfort them with the hope of the light eternal, to which, of thy great mercy, we beseech thee to bring us all; through Jesus Christ our Saviour.

O HELPER of the helpless, we ask thy compassion for all who are in necessity and need thy succour: for orphans and widows; for all in prison or under sentence of death; for those in despair or tempted to suicide; and for all in bitter servitude or insane. Bless them, O Lord, and shew the light of thy countenance upon them all.

FATHER, give us grace not to pass by suffering or joy without eyes to see: give us understanding and wise sympathy, and preserve us from clumsiness, that we may be sorry with those who weep and glad with those who rejoice. Use us, as thou canst, to make happy and strong the hearts of others, and humbly to set forth thy light which is the light of the world.

O GOD, the strength of them that labour and the rest of the weary: grant us, when we are tired, to be refreshed by thy Spirit; that, being made fit for the service of thy Kingdom, we may serve thee gladly in freshness of body and mind; through Jesus Christ our Lord.

MERCIFULLY look upon us, O God, and grant us such health of body as thou knowest to be needful for us: that we may faithfully serve thee with all our being, and throughout our lives.

O MERCIFUL God, grant that all worldly affections may die in us, and that all things belonging to the Spirit may live and grow in us. Grant that we may have power and strength to have victory and to triumph against the devil, the world, and the flesh. Grant that we, who are dedicated to thee, may also be endued with heavenly virtues; through thy mercy, O blessed Lord God, who dost live, and govern all things, world without end.

THE God of peace himself sanctify you wholly; and may your spirit and soul and body be preserved entire, without blame at the coming of our Lord Jesus Christ. *Amen.*

HYMNS

A. & M.	S.P.	
254		Art thou weary, art thou languid?
238	449	As pants the hart for cooling streams
	461	Can I see another's woe?
	509	Happy are they, they that love God
176	527	How sweet the name of Jesus sounds
266	554	Lead, kindly Light, amid the encircling gloom

XV

WHILE WE WERE YET SINNERS

Thou shalt call his name Jesus; for it is he that shall save his people from their sins.

BLESSED be God, the creator, preserver, and governor of all things, King of kings and Lord of lords: who, though he hath his dwelling so high, yet humbleth himself to behold the things which are in heaven and earth. O give thanks unto the Lord, for he is gracious: and his mercy endureth for ever.

ALMIGHTY and most merciful God, we acknowledge and confess that we have sinned against thee in thought, and word, and deed: that we have not loved thee with all our heart and soul, with all our mind and strength; and that we have not loved our neighbours as ourselves. We beseech thee, O God, to be forgiving to what we have been, to help us to amend what we are, and of thy mercy to direct what we shall be; so that the love of goodness may ever be first in our hearts, and we may follow unto our lives' end in the steps of Jesus Christ our Lord.

O GOD who, by thy Son Jesus Christ, hast brought forgiveness and reconciliation to men, grant to us sinners thy pardon and peace. Turn thee again, O Lord, at the last, and be gracious unto thy servants; for his sake who died and rose again for us, thy Son Jesus Christ our Lord.

OUR FATHER . . .

PSALM

51, 1–12. Have mercy upon me, O God, after thy great
goodness

142. I cried unto the Lord with my voice

OUR Father, in these hours of daylight we remember
those who must wake that we may sleep: bless those
who watch over us at night, the firemen and police, and
all who carry on through the hours of darkness the restless commerce of men on land and sea. We thank thee
for their faithfulness and sense of duty; we pray thee for
pardon, if our selfishness or luxury adds to their nightly
toil. Grant that we may realize how dependent the safety
of our loved ones and the comforts of life are on these our
brothers, that so we may think of them with love and
gratitude, and help to make their burden lighter; for the
sake of Jesus Christ our Lord.

ALMIGHTY God, we beseech thee to hear our prayers
for such as sin against thee, or neglect to serve thee:
that thou wouldest bestow upon them true repentance,
and an earnest longing for thy service; through Jesus
Christ our Lord.

O LORD, who hast brought us through the darkness of
night to the light of the morning, and who by thy
Holy Spirit dost illumine the darkness of ignorance and
sin: we beseech thee, of thy loving-kindness, to pour thy
holy light into our souls, that we may ever be devoted to
thee, by whose wisdom we were created, by whose mercy
we were redeemed, and by whose providence we are
governed; to the honour and glory of thy name.

THOU knowest, O heavenly Father, the duties that lie before us this day, the dangers that may confront us, the sins that most beset us. Guide us, strengthen us, protect us. Give us thy life in such abundance that we may this day hold our souls in thy pure light. Give us thy power, that we may become a power for righteousness among our fellows. Give us thy love, that all lesser things may have no attraction for us; that selfishness, impurity, and falseness may drop away as dead desires, holding no meaning for us. Let us find thy power, thy love, thy life, in all mankind, and in the secret places of our own souls.

DELIVER us, O God, from all evil and mischief: from all blindness of heart, from pride, vain-glory, and hypocrisy; from envy, hatred, and malice, and all uncharitableness; for the sake of thy Son, Jesus Christ our Lord.

O THOU who searchest the hearts of men, look with mercy upon our sins against thy truth: forgive them for Jesus' sake; and help us to walk in the light this day. Deliver us from timid or sullen silence; give us grace to speak with simple truth and open kindness; and so dwell in our hearts by thy Spirit of truth that thought, word, and deed may be made one in love.

O GOD our Father, help us this day to speak and to do only such things as will leave no regret. Grant us reverence for all that is good; teach us to hate all that is selfish and base. In our dealings with our fellows, inspire in us the spirit of courtesy and goodwill. Make us strong to control our desires, and resolute to match our action to our highest thought; through Jesus Christ our Lord.

O ALMIGHTY Lord and everlasting God, vouchsafe, we beseech thee, to direct, sanctify, and govern both our hearts and bodies, in the ways of thy laws, and in the works of thy commandments: that through thy most mighty protection, both here and ever, we may be preserved in body and soul; through our Lord and Saviour Jesus Christ.

O GOD, set our hearts at liberty from the service of ourselves: and let it be our meat and drink to serve others and to do thy will.

U NTO him that loveth us, and loosed us from our sins by his blood; and he made us to be a kingdom, to be priests unto his God and Father; to him be the glory and the dominion for ever and ever. *Amen.*

HYMNS

A. & . M.	S.P.	
3[(2)]	25[(3)]	Glory to thee, who safe hast kept
255	253	Just as I am, without one plea
184	636	Rock of ages, cleft for me
248	118	Shepherd divine, our wants relieve
181		We know thee, who thou art
	Par. 60	Father of peace, and God of love!

XVI

SUFFERED UNDER PONTIUS PILATE

That I may know him, and the fellowship of his sufferings.
Insomuch as ye are partakers of Christ's sufferings, rejoice.

O FATHER of our Lord Jesus Christ, who didst graciously send thy Son to suffer and die for us men and for our salvation: make us truly thankful for this and all thy benefits.

For thy long-suffering with the sins and sorrows of men from the beginning even until now:

For the sufferings of Christ in the flesh, and his intercession for mankind in glory:

For the redemption of the world through the pain of the Passion and the shame of the Cross:

For all who have filled up the sufferings of Christ in their own lives for love of him and of their fellow men:

We thank thee, O God.

BLESSED Lord, who wast content for our sakes to bear sorrow and want and death: grant to us such a measure of thy Spirit that we may follow thee in all self-denial and tenderness of soul. Help us, by thy great love, to succour the afflicted, to relieve the needy and destitute, to comfort the feeble-minded, to share the burdens of the heavy-laden, and ever to see thee in all that are poor and desolate.

OUR FATHER . . .

PSALM

32. Blessed is he whose unrighteousness is forgiven

16. Preserve me, O God

ALMIGHTY God, who art afflicted in the afflictions of thy people, and art full of compassion and tender mercy: hear us as we pray for all who are in trouble; for those who have lost the health and strength that once was theirs; for those who are trying bravely to face illness and suffering:

For all who are handicapped in the race of life through no fault of their own; for the defective and delicate and the permanently injured:

For those who lie in pain; for any who have to undergo an operation; for the blind, the deaf, and the dumb; and for all who have to watch their loved ones suffer:

For those whose livelihood is insecure; for the hungry, the homeless, and the destitute; for those who have the will to work, but lack the opportunity of working:

For those who have to bear their burdens alone, and for all who have lost those whom they love:

For those who are in doubt or anguish of soul; for those who are victims of depression, anxiety, and fear; for those whose suffering is unrelieved by the knowledge of thy love.

And we thank thee, O Father, for all who hallow pain: for those whose thought is always for others; for those whose faith brings light to the dark places of life; for those whose patience inspires others to endure. And grant, O loving Father, to all who are bound in the mysterious fellowship of suffering, the sense of comradeship with others and the knowledge of thy love; and give them thy peace which passes all understanding.

O GOD of light and peace, give light and peace to them that are of a troubled mind. Grant them courage and patience, that they may seek for the causes of their ills; and give wisdom to those who help them to do so. And, for those whose sufferings continue, we pray that they may be cared for in love, and that none may add to their griefs. We ask this in the name of him who succoured the distressed, thy son Jesus Christ our Lord.

WE sinners do beseech thee, O God, that it may please thee to give to all nations unity, peace, and concord: to give us a heart to love and fear thee, and diligently to live after thy commandments; to bring into the way of truth all such as have erred and are deceived; to strengthen such as do stand; to comfort and help the weak-hearted; to raise up them that fall; and finally to beat down Satan under our feet.

COMFORT, we beseech thee, most gracious God, all who are cast down and faint of heart amid the sickness and sorrow of the world: and grant that, by the power of thy Holy Spirit, they may be enabled to go on their way rejoicing; through Jesus Christ our Lord.

O LORD Jesus Christ, Son of the living God, who wast led forth to the pain of the Cross for the salvation of the world: we humbly beseech thee that, by the virtue of thy most sacred Passion, thou wouldest blot out all our sins, and mercifully bring us to the glory of thy blessedness; who livest and reignest, God world without end.

O SAVIOUR of the world, who by thy Cross and Passion hast redeemed us: save us and help us, we humbly beseech thee, O Lord.

THE God of all grace, who called you unto his eternal glory in Christ, after that ye have suffered a little while, shall himself perfect, stablish, strengthen you. To him be the dominion for ever and ever. *Amen.*

HYMNS

A. & M.	S.P.	
112		All ye who seek for sure relief
189		Jesu, thy mercies are untold
549	113	O for a heart to praise my God
699		O Love, that wilt not let me go
172	625	Praise to the Holiest in the height
180		To Christ, the Prince of peace

XVII

THEY CRUCIFIED HIM

I, if I be lifted up from the earth, will draw all men unto myself.

GLORY be to thee, O Lord, who, having become obedient unto death, even the death of the Cross, art highly exalted: and hast opened unto us the gate of everlasting life. Therefore unto thee every knee shall bow, and every tongue shall confess thee Lord of all, to the glory of God the Father. We adore thee, O Christ, and we praise thee: because by thy Cross and Passion thou hast redeemed the world.

O CHRIST, the true vine and the source of life, ever giving thyself that the world may live: who also hast taught us that those who would follow thee must be ready to lose their lives for thy sake; grant us so to receive within our souls the power of thine eternal sacrifice, that in sharing thy cup we may share thy glory, and at the last be made perfect in thy love.

OUR FATHER . . .

PSALM

22, 1–11. My God, my God, look upon me; why hast thou forsaken me?

40, 1–12. I waited patiently for the Lord

REMEMBER, O God our Father, every faithful soul in trial: and comfort every one in sorrow and distress. O helper of the helpless, bring the wanderer home; give health to the sick, and deliverance to the captive. Sustain the aged, comfort the weak-hearted, set free those whose

F

souls are bound in misery and iron. Let us dwell with thee in peace, as children of light; and in thy light let us see light. Direct in peace the close of our life; trustfully, fearlessly, and, if it be thy will, painlessly. Gather us when thou wilt into the abodes of thy chosen, without shame or sin; for Jesus Christ's sake.

L ORD Jesus, we beseech thee by the loneliness of thy suffering on the Cross, be nigh unto all who are desolate and in pain or sorrow to-day: and let thy presence transform their loneliness into comfort, consolation, and holy fellowship with thee, thou pitiful Saviour.

O LORD Jesus, who on the Cross didst bear the weight of bodily pain: may we learn from thee how to bear pain, lest we grow self-absorbed, self-pitying, or self-indulgent. Teach us to receive graciously the care and relief which others offer to us, to be willing to be dependent when we can no longer work for ourselves; and through all our struggles in weakness and suffering may we share in the victory of the spirit over the flesh, to thy honour and glory.

A LMIGHTY and everlasting God, who of thy tender love towards mankind hast sent thy Son our Saviour Jesus Christ, to take upon him our flesh, and to suffer death upon the Cross, that all mankind should follow the example of his great humility: mercifully grant that we may both follow the example of his patience, and also be made partakers of his resurrection; through the same Jesus Christ our Lord.

O LORD who, when thine hour was come, didst go without fear among those that sought thy life: give us such boldness to confess thee before men, that hereafter thou mayest confess us before thy Father who is in heaven; and grant us to inherit an eternal crown.

ALMIGHTY God, who hast shewn us in the life and teaching of thy Son the true way of blessedness, and in his suffering and death that the path of love may lead to the Cross, and the reward of faithfulness may be a crown of thorns: give us grace to take up our cross and follow Christ, and to have such fellowship with him in his sorrow that we may learn the secret of his strength and peace; and may see, even in our darkest hour of trial, the shining of the eternal light.

O LORD, give us more charity, more self-denial, more likeness to thee. Teach us to sacrifice our comforts to others, and our desires for the sake of doing good. Make us kindly in thought, gentle in word, generous in deed. Teach us that it is better to minister than to be ministered unto; better to give than to receive; better to forget ourselves than to put ourselves forward. And unto thee, O Lord of love, be glory and praise for ever.

O MERCIFUL Lord Jesus Christ, who didst commend thy spirit into the hands of thy heavenly Father: so assist us, we beseech thee, by thy most precious death, that at the hour of our departing from this mortal life we may be received into thine everlasting Kingdom, there to reign with thee, world without end.

ALMIGHTY God, who seest that we have no power of ourselves to help ourselves: keep us both outwardly in our bodies, and inwardly in our souls; that we may be defended from all adversities which may happen to the body, and from all evil thoughts which may assault and hurt the soul; through Jesus Christ our Lord.

REMEMBER, O God, what thou hast wrought in us and not what we deserve: and, as thou hast called us to thy service, make us worthy of our calling; through Jesus Christ our Lord.

To God the Father, who loved us, and made us accepted in the Beloved: to God the Son, who loved us, and loosed us from our sins by his own blood: to God the Holy Ghost, who sheddeth the love of God abroad in our hearts: to the one true God be all love and all glory, for time and for eternity. *Amen.*

HYMNS

A. & M.	S.P.	
106	110	My God, I love thee; not because
277	586	Nearer, my God, to thee
263	119	Take up thy cross, the Saviour said
332	131	There is a green hill far away
200	132	We sing the praise of him who died
108	133	When I survey the wondrous Cross

XVIII

ALIVE FOR EVERMORE

That I(we) may know him, and the power of his resurrection.

BLESSED be the God and Father of our Lord Jesus Christ, who according to his great mercy begat us again unto a living hope by the resurrection of Jesus Christ from the dead. Worthy is the Lamb that was slain to receive power, and riches, and wisdom, and strength, and honour, and glory, and blessing, now and for evermore.

————

WE give thanks to thee, O heavenly Father, who, by the appearing of thy Son Jesus Christ to his disciples after his crucifixion, hast made known to us that death has no dominion over him, and that with him we may enter through death into life eternal. We praise thee, O Christ, who hast made dying to be the pathway into the fuller life. Thou, O Christ, hast taken from us the fear of death, and by that path we would follow thee into that realm of glorious living, where thou art: for eye has not seen, nor ear heard, the things which thou hast prepared for them that love thee. We praise thee, O Holy Spirit of Christ, who bearest witness with our spirits that we are the children of God; and if children, then heirs; heirs of God, and joint-heirs with Christ; if so be that we suffer with him, that we may be also glorified with him.

OUR FATHER . . .   P.T.O

PSALM

118, 5-18. I called upon the Lord in trouble

114. When Israel came out of Egypt

O GOD our Father, who hast bidden the light to shine out of darkness, and hast again wakened us to praise thy goodness and ask for thy grace: accept now the offering of our worship and thanksgiving, and grant unto us all such requests as may be good for us. Make us to be children of the light and of the day, and heirs of thine everlasting inheritance. Remember, according to the multitude of thy mercies, thy whole Church; all who join with us in prayer; all our brethren in any country who stand in need of thy grace and succour. Pour out upon them the riches of thy mercy; so that, being redeemed in soul and body and steadfast in faith, we may ever praise thy wonderful and holy name; through Jesus Christ our Lord.

ALMIGHTY God, who hast taught us to make prayers and intercessions for all men:—

We pray to thee for ministers of religion, and all who guide the thoughts of the people; for artists, authors, musicians, and journalists; that our common life may be crowned with truth and beauty: *O Lord etc.*

For all who heal the body, guard the health of the people, and tend the sick; that they may follow in the footsteps of Christ, the great physician: *O Lord etc.*

For all, on whose labour we depend for the necessaries of life; for those who carry on the commerce of the world, that they may seek no private gain which would hinder the good of all: *O Lord etc.*

For parents and children; that purity, love, and honour may dwell in our homes, and duty and affection may be the bond of our family life: *O Lord etc.*

For the weak in body and mind, that they may be restored to health; for those who are depressed and in pain, that they may be helped and comforted: *O Lord etc.*

For all who draw nigh unto death, that they may know thy presence with them through the valley of the shadow, and may awake to behold thy face. *O Lord etc.*

O FATHER of all, we remember before thee those whom we love but see no longer. Grant them thy peace; let light perpetual shine upon them; and in thy loving wisdom and almighty power work in them the good purpose of thy perfect will; through Jesus Christ our Lord.

ALMIGHTY God who, through thine only-begotten Son Jesus Christ, hast overcome death and opened unto us the gate of everlasting life: we humbly beseech thee that, as by thy special grace directing us, thou dost put into our minds good desires, so by thy continual help we may bring the same to good effect; through Jesus Christ our Lord, who liveth and reigneth with thee and the Holy Spirit, ever one God, world without end.

O GOD who, through the mighty resurrection of thy Son Jesus Christ from the dead, hast delivered us from the power of darkness and brought us into the Kingdom of thy love: grant, we beseech thee, that, as by his death he has recalled us to life, so by his presence ever abiding in us he may raise us to joys eternal; through the same Jesus Christ our Lord.

GRANT unto us, O God, the royalty of inward happiness, and the serenity which comes from living close to thee. Daily renew in us the sense of joy, and let thy Spirit

dwell in our hearts; that we may bear about with us the
infection of a good courage, and may meet all life's ills
and accidents with gallant and high-hearted happiness,
giving thee thanks always for all things; through Jesus
Christ our Lord.

THE God of peace, who brought again from the dead
the great shepherd of the sheep with the blood of the
eternal covenant, even our Lord Jesus, make you perfect
in every good thing to do his will, working in us that
which is well-pleasing in his sight, through Jesus Christ; O L.
to whom be the glory for ever and ever. *Amen.*

HYMNS

A. & M.	S.P.	
	435	A brighter dawn is breaking
137	150	Alleluia! Alleluia! Hearts to heaven and voices raise
302		Come, ye faithful, raise the anthem
232	199	Light's abode, celestial Salem
224	599	O happy band of pilgrims
125		Ye choirs of new Jerusalem
	Par. 61	Bless'd be the everlasting God

XIX

I reckon that the sufferings of this present time are not worthy to be compared with the glory which shall be revealed to usward.

And there shall be night no more; and they need no light of lamp, neither light of sun; for the Lord God shall give them light: and they shall reign for ever and ever.

WE offer to thee, O God, our praise and adoration: who, through the glorious resurrection of thy Son Jesus Christ, hast given unto us an inheritance incorruptible and undefiled, reserved in heaven for us; who hast blessed us with all spiritual blessings in Christ; who comfortest us in all tribulation. Unto thee be praise, might, majesty, dominion, and power, both now and for ever.

O ETERNAL God, who hast ever been and ever wilt be: to thee we bring the wants which none but thyself can satisfy, and the unquiet hearts which thou alone canst still. To us belong the courses of continual change; we pass through the darkness and the light of this world, but thou art ever the same. Only in imperfect and broken accents can we utter thy praise, but we would cast ourselves before thee and join in the song of the ages. Glory be to thee, O Lord most high.

OUR FATHER . . .

PSALM

57. Be merciful unto me, O God, be merciful unto me, for my soul trusteth in thee

116, 1–9. I am well pleased

O GOD, before whose face the generations rise and pass away, the strength of those who labour and suffer, and the repose of the holy and blessed dead: we rejoice in the communion of thy saints. We remember all who have faithfully lived and died, and especially those most dear to us. Lift us into light and love; give us at last our portion with those who have trusted in thee, and have striven in all things to do thy will. And to thy name, with the Church on earth and the Church in heaven, we ascribe all honour and glory.

O LOVING Father, who seest all the suffering, injustice, and misery, which abound in this world: look mercifully upon the poor, the oppressed, and all who are heavy laden with labour, or sorrow, or ignorance. Fill our hearts with deep compassion for those who suffer, and hasten the coming of thy Kingdom of justice and truth; for the sake of Jesus Christ our Lord.

GOD of our life, help us in the days when the burdens we carry chafe our shoulders and weigh us down: when the road seems dreary and endless, the skies grey and threatening; when our lives have no music in them, our hearts are lonely, and our souls have lost their courage. Flood the path with light, we beseech thee; turn our eyes to where the skies are full of promise; tune our hearts to brave music; bind us in comradeship with the heroes and saints of every age; and so quicken our spirits that we may be able to encourage the souls of all who journey with us on the road of life; to thy honour and glory.

ALMIGHTY Father, the source from which we come, the end to which we travel, and the light and strength of our pilgrimage: mercifully grant that at the last all that is good in us may prevail over what is evil; that everything may be brought into harmony with thy will, and that thou mayest be all in all. We ask it in the name of him who declared thy gracious purposes to mankind, thy Son Jesus Christ our Lord.

O GOD, in whom alone we find rest from our weariness and comfort for our sorrow, and from whom alone comes all true joy: keep our hearts, we beseech thee, ever fixed on thee through life and death, waiting patiently for that glorious day when we shall rejoice in the fulness of thy love for evermore.

O ALMIGHTY God, who hast knit together thine elect in one communion and fellowship, in the mystical body of thy Son Christ our Lord: grant us grace so to follow thy blessed saints in all virtuous and godly living, that we may come to those unspeakable joys which thou hast prepared for them that unfeignedly love thee; through Jesus Christ our Lord.

ALMIGHTY God, who hast given thine only Son to be unto us both a sacrifice for sin, and also an example of godly life: give us grace that we may always most thankfully receive that his inestimable benefit, and also daily endeavour ourselves to follow the blessed steps of his most holy life; through the same Jesus Christ our Lord.

O GOD who, by the glorious death and resurrection of thy Son Jesus Christ, hast brought life and immortality to light: grant us so to die daily unto sin that we may evermore live with thee in the joy of his resurrection; through the same Jesus Christ our Lord, to whom be glory and dominion for ever and ever.

Bestow upon us, O God our Father, understanding to know thee: diligence to seek thee, wisdom to find thee, and a faithfulness that may finally embrace thee; through Jesus Christ our Lord.

To Jesus Christ, who is the faithful witness, the first-born of the dead, and the ruler of the kings of the earth, be the glory and the dominion for ever and ever. *Amen.*

HYMNS

A. & M.	S.P.	
547	463	Children of the heavenly King
231	195	'For ever with the Lord!'
	514	He wants not friends that hath thy love
236		Jerusalem, my happy home
535	105	Lord, it belongs not to my care
222		Ten thousand times ten thousand

XX

LIFT UP YOUR HEARTS

*If then ye were raised together with Christ, seek the things that
are above, where Christ is, seated on the right hand of God.*

GLORY to our ascended Lord, that he is with us always:
glory to the Word of God, going forth conquering
and to conquer; glory to him who has led captivity
captive, and gone before to prepare a place in his Father's
house for us, the author and finisher of our faith. And
may God in all things be glorified, through Jesus Christ,
to whom be worship and praise, now and for ever.

HOLY, righteous, and merciful God: that we may offer
thee true worship and joyful service, cleanse our
minds and free our consciences from the things that hide
thee from us, and grant us the help of thy grace. On our
blindness to thy glory and forgetfulness of thy truth; on
our unwillingness to be guided by thy Spirit; on our
failures in love and on our pride; on our denials of thee
in life's common ways; O Lord, have mercy.

For the pardon and joy that is ours in Christ Jesus let
us give thanks unto God, and say:

OUR FATHER . . .

PSALM

24. The earth is the Lord's, and all that therein is

20. The Lord hear thee in the day of trouble

O LORD, the protector of our lives, thou hast shielded
us while we slept, and in thy mercy hast awakened
us once more. And now in the morning of a new day
we lift up our voices unto thee, beseeching thee to be as

the freshness of the dawn upon our hearts, that at thy touch every cloud may flee away. May we take up our duties with glad and willing minds; so that, whatever burdens the day shall lay upon us, we may bear them in thy strength; that, whatever joys the day shall bring, we may receive and rejoice in them with thanksgiving unto thee, from whom they came; that we may live this day and all our days not for ourselves only, but for others; that if there be any who turn to us in their need, in sin, sickness, or sorrow, we may bring help, consolation, and loving-kindness to them as unto thy children, O Lord, whose goodness knoweth no end, and whose very name is Love.

O GOD, who art present in every place and from whose love no space or distance can ever separate us: grant us to know that those who are absent from one another are still present with thee; and, though separated, may we realize our fellowship with one another in our common service of thee; through Jesus Christ our Lord.

O CHRIST, our Saviour, the strength of the weak, the friend of sinners, and the comfort of the sorrowful: grant thy mighty protection to the tempted; reveal thy grace to the fallen; maintain the faith of those who are persecuted for righteousness' sake; and give the consolation of thy presence to all who are disappointed, embittered, lonely, or in despair; for thy tender mercy's sake.

GRANT, we beseech thee, almighty God, that, like as we do believe thine only-begotten Son our Lord Jesus Christ to have ascended into the heavens, so we may also in heart and mind thither ascend, and with him continually dwell; who liveth and reigneth with thee and the Holy Ghost, one God, world without end.

ALMIGHTY God, unto whom all hearts are open, all desires known, and from whom no secrets are hid: cleanse the thoughts of our hearts by the inspiration of thy Holy Spirit, that we may perfectly love thee, and worthily magnify thy holy name; through Christ our Lord.

SET free, O God, our souls from all restlessness and anxiety: give us that peace and power which flow from thee. Keep us in all perplexities and distresses, in all fears and faithlessness; that so, upheld by thy power and stayed on the rock of thy faithfulness, we may through storm and stress abide in thee; through Jesus Christ our Lord.

O LORD Jesus Christ, who art the way, the truth, and the life: suffer us not, we pray thee, to wander from thee who art the way, nor to distrust thee who art the truth, nor to rest in any other than thee who art the life. Teach us what to do, what to believe, and wherein to take our rest.

ALMIGHTY and everlasting God, who makest us both to will and to do those things that are good and acceptable unto thee: we beseech thee so to lead us in the knowledge of thy truth and obedience to thy will, that out of weakness we may be made strong, and even now may enter into life eternal.

O GOD the King of glory, who hast exalted thine only Son Jesus Christ with great triumph unto thy Kingdom in heaven: we beseech thee, leave us not comfortless, but send to us thy Holy Ghost to comfort us, and exalt us unto the same place whither our Saviour Christ is gone before; who liveth and reigneth with thee and the Holy Ghost, one God, world without end.

MAY God the Holy Spirit, through his grace, build us up in faith and truth and love, that we may have our portion among the saints with all those who believe in our Lord Jesus Christ. *Amen.*

HYMNS

A. & M.	S.P.	
304		Crown him with many crowns
150		Jesu, our hope, our heart's desire
178(2)		O Jesu, King most wonderful
167	618	O worship the King all glorious above
202	632	Rejoice! The Lord is King
301	175	The head that once was crowned with thorns
	Par. 30	Come, let us to the Lord our God

XXI

MY LORD AND MY GOD

Have this mind in you, which was also in Christ Jesus: who, being found in fashion as a man, humbled himself, becoming obedient even unto death, yea, the death of the cross. Wherefore also God highly exalted him, and gave unto him the name which is above every name; that in the name of Jesus every knee should bow.

WE worship thee, O Lord God, and give thanks to thee for the great glory and power which thou shewest to thy servants in thy wonderful works. All that we enjoy is from thy mighty hand, and thou alone art to be praised for the blessings of this life. Make us thankful to thee for all thy mercies, and more ready to serve thee with all our hearts; for the sake of Jesus Christ our Lord.

O LORD our God, almighty and everlasting, to whom belong all those secret things which the mind of man cannot yet comprehend: we thank thee for the truths thou hast revealed, which belong to us and to our children for ever. We thank thee that thy word is not hidden from us, neither is it far off, but in our hearts, that we may obey it; we thank thee that thy will is written in our consciences, that we may do it. May we love thee with all our heart, with all our mind, with all our soul and with all our strength, and love our neighbours as ourselves, and so fulfil the law of Christ; to whom be glory and praise for ever.

OUR FATHER . . .

G

PSALM

1. Blessed is the man that hath not walked in the counsel of the ungodly, nor stood in the way of sinners

72, 1–8, 17–19. Give the king thy judgments, O God

O ETERNAL God, in whose will is our peace, we commend to thee the needs of all the world. Where there is hatred, give love; where there is injury, pardon; where there is doubt, faith; where there is despair, hope; where there is darkness, light; where there is sadness, joy. May we ourselves seek not so much to be consoled as to console; to be understood as to understand; to be loved as to love. For it is in giving that we receive; it is in pardoning that we are pardoned; it is in dying that we are born to eternal life in thy blessed Son, Jesus Christ our Lord.

O LORD God of hosts, stretch forth, we pray thee, thine almighty arm to strengthen and protect the forces of our King in every peril of land, and sea, and air: endue them with loyalty and courage; shelter them in the day of battle, and in time of peace keep them safe from all evil; through Jesus Christ our Lord.

O HEAVENLY Father, who dost mercifully remember those who abide at home, as well as those who go out to the world's business: cheer them in their daily toil, uphold them through any worries or anxieties that may oppress them; be their companion in all their tasks, and give them strength for their work and peace in doing it.

O GOD, the true light of believers, the eternal glory of the just: as thou hast brought us through the night to the morning of a new day, so lead us at length to that blessed and everlasting day where night is no more; where thou art glorified by thy saints, and adored by all them that believe.

O GOD, who hast called us thy servants into the glorious liberty of the sons of God: grant that we may not refuse from cowardice thy gifts of freedom, nor use them to hurt or maim the lives of others, or for our own selfish ends. In thy service may we find our perfect freedom, O God, our Redeemer and our King.

O GOD our Father, shew thou us the way that we should walk in, for we lift up our souls unto thee: keep our feet upon that strait and narrow way which will lead us to the more abundant life. When we hunger for a fuller life, be thou to us the living bread: when our spirits are parched, be thou within us a spring of living water, refreshing the dry surfaces of life. When we look forward with dread to the days that are to come, shew thyself to us as our exceeding great reward. Teach us that the lovely things of life can never be taken away, for they are all in thee and thou in them; and that no power can sever us from the blessed companionship of love, until we wake up after thy likeness and are satisfied with it in thy Kingdom, where all good things are fulfilled and continued in thee, O Father of everlasting love.

O JESUS our master, who didst shew unfailing patience and gentleness in thy judgment of the people round thee: keep us from the careless criticism and the unkind gossip which cause so much suffering to others; help us to think and to speak of every one with fairness and charity. We ask it for thy sake.

O GOD, who hast taught us that all our doings without love are nothing worth: send thy Holy Spirit and pour into our hearts that most excellent gift of love, the very bond of peace and of all virtues, without which whosoever liveth is counted dead before thee; grant this for thine only Son Jesus Christ's sake.

GRANT unto us, O God, so to pass this day in thy holy service that the obedience of our lives may be acceptable unto thee: give thy angels charge over us, to keep us in all our ways. And, since in Christ thou didst come to save the lost, let not one of us whom thou hast redeemed perish through sin or neglect. We ask this in the name of Jesus Christ our Saviour.

UNTO the King eternal, incorruptible, invisible, the only God, be honour and glory for ever and ever. *Amen.*

HYMNS

A. & M.	S.P.	
79	83	As with gladness men of old
514	252	Father of all, to thee
655	528	I bind unto myself to-day
	537	In Christ there is no East or West
193	542	Jesu, lover of my soul
	652	Teach me, my God and King
Par.	54	I'm not ashamed to own my Lord

XXII

LORD OF ALL

Go ye therefore, and make disciples of all the nations, baptizing them into the name of the Father and of the Son and of the Holy Ghost: teaching them to observe all things whatsoever I commanded you.

WORTHY art thou, O God, to receive power, and riches, and wisdom, and strength, and honour, and glory, and blessing: salvation to our God, which sitteth upon the throne, and to the Lamb, for ever and ever. We bless thee, heavenly Father, that nothing can separate us from the love of Christ; that in tribulation, or distress, or persecution, or famine, or nakedness, or peril, or sword, in all these things we are more than conquerors through him that loved us.

O FATHER of men, who hast promised that the kingdoms of this world shall become the Kingdom of thy Son: purge the nations of error and corruption; overthrow the power of sin, and establish the Kingdom of grace in every land. Incline the hearts of all rulers and peoples to the Lord of lords and King of glory, that he may enter into their cities, churches, and homes, to dwell there, and govern all things by his Word and Spirit.

OUR FATHER . . .

PSALM

67. God be merciful unto us, and bless us

95, 1-7. O come, let us sing unto the Lord

ALMIGHTY God, who rulest in the kingdom of men, and hast given to our Sovereign Lord, King George, a great dominion in all parts of the earth: draw together, we pray thee, in true fellowship the men of divers races, languages, and customs, who dwell therein; that, bearing one another's burdens and working together in brotherly concord, they may fulfil the purpose of thy providence, and set forward thine everlasting Kingdom. Pardon, we beseech thee, our sins and shortcomings; keep far from us all selfishness and pride; and give us grace to employ thy good gifts of order and freedom to thy glory and the welfare of mankind; through Jesus Christ thy Son our Lord, to whom with thee and the Holy Ghost be all glory and dominion, world without end.

GRANT us, O God, a vision of our land, fair as she might be: a land of justice, where none shall prey on others; a land of plenty, where vice and poverty shall cease to fester; a land of brotherhood, where success shall be founded on service, and honour shall be given to worth alone; a land of peace, where order shall not rest on force, but on the love of all for their land, the great mother of the common life and welfare. Hear thou, O Lord, the silent prayer of all our hearts as in city, town, and village, we pledge our time and strength and thought, to hasten the day of her coming beauty and righteousness.

O GOD, by whose will we were born to be citizens of this land, enable us to love our country not in word only, but also in deed and in truth. Let us never rejoice in any pleasures that do harm to others, nor accept a life of idleness while others toil for our comfort. Let those

who have most received be ready most to give, in the
spirit of thy Son Jesus Christ our Lord.

ALMIGHTY God, who dost sanctify with thy Spirit the
common ways of life: give to us and to all who
use the roads the spirit of courtesy and goodwill, of
carefulness and self-control; that, by our thought for
others, we may all be preserved from needless danger and
sudden death, and may live to glorify thee in our going
out and our coming in; through Jesus Christ our Lord.

O GOD, the Lord of all kings and kingdoms, let thy
strong hand control the nations, and cause them to
long for thy love to rule on the earth. Strengthen, we
pray thee, all who are striving after true brotherhood
and who are working for righteousness and peace. Guide
the hearts and minds of rulers and statesmen, that they
may seek first thy Kingdom and the establishing of justice
and freedom for all peoples, both great and small. We
ask this for Christ's sake.

O GOD, the Father of our Lord Jesus Christ, our only
Saviour, the Prince of peace: give us grace seriously
to lay to heart the great dangers we are in by our unhappy
divisions. Take away all hatred and prejudice, and whatever else may hinder us from godly union and concord;
that, as there is but one body and one Spirit, and one
hope of our calling, one Lord, one faith, one baptism,
one God and Father of us all, so we may henceforth be
all of one heart and of one soul, united in one holy bond
of truth and peace, of faith and charity; and may with one
mind and one mouth glorify thee; through Jesus Christ
our Lord.

O GOD our Father, in whom is calmness, peace, and concord: heal, we pray thee, the dissensions which divide the nations of the world from one another, and bring us into a unity of love in Jesus Christ our Lord.

ETERNAL Father, from whom every family in heaven and earth is named, who didst send thy Son to seek and to save that which was lost: we pray, in hope of thy mercy, for all souls whom thou hast made; that they may be gathered home to thee at last in one unbroken family, the lost found and the rebellious reconciled; through Jesus Christ our Saviour.

THE Lord of peace himself give you peace at all times in all ways. The Lord be with you all. *Amen.*

HYMNS

A. & M.	S.P.	
306	392	At the name of Jesus
	64	Hills of the North, rejoice
529	551	Jesus, where'er thy people meet
	322	O beautiful, my country
217		Thy Kingdom come, O God
166	443	All people that on earth do dwell
	M.P. 100	

XXIII

FOR THE HEALING OF THE NATIONS

Nations shall come to thy light, and kings to the brightness of thy rising.

They shall bring the glory and the honour of the nations into it.

FROM the rising of the sun to the going down of the same, the Lord's name is to be praised. O Emmanuel, the desire of all nations and their Saviour, come and save us, O Lord our God.

Thanks be to thee, most glorious God, Father, Son, and Holy Spirit, for the revelation of thyself to our world, and for the commission to thy disciples to proclaim the gospel of Christ to every creature.

Praise be to thy name for the first disciples who were sent forth to proclaim the coming of his Kingdom; for the apostles who, in obedience to his word, carried the gospel to many lands; for the messengers, known and unknown, who brought the good tidings to these shores; for those who in the ages of darkness kept alive the light, and who, while men slumbered and slept, were faithful to their Lord's command; for those who have gone to the ends of the world with the joyful news, and have sought out the dark places of the earth, to give light to them that dwell in the shadow of death; for thy missionary servants who have joined the noble army of martyrs, and for all converts to the faith who have sealed their witness with their blood; for the innumerable company who now praise thy name, out of every kindred and nation and tongue.

OUR FATHER . . .

PSALM

TE DEUM, 1–21. We praise thee, O God

42, 1–7, 14, 15. Like as the hart desireth the water-brooks

O GOD, who hast made of one blood all nations of men to dwell on the face of the earth, and didst send thy blessed son, Jesus Christ, to preach peace to them that are far off, and to them that are nigh: grant that all the peoples of the world may feel after thee and find thee; and hasten, O Lord, the fulfilment of thy promise to pour out thy Spirit upon all flesh; through Jesus Christ our Lord.

O GOD, who art the lover of justice and peace: give thy grace, we humbly beseech thee, to those who now guide the League of Nations; and so lead them by thy Holy Spirit that by word and deed they may promote thy glory, and set forward peace and goodwill among men.

O GOD, our heavenly Father, who didst manifest thy love by sending thine only-begotten Son into the world, that all might live through him: pour thy Spirit upon thy Church, that it may fulfil his command to preach the gospel to every creature; send forth, we beseech thee, labourers into thy harvest; defend them in dangers and temptations, and hasten the time when all shall be saved; through the same thy Son Jesus Christ our Lord.

O GOD, the physician of men and nations, the restorer of the years that have been destroyed: look upon the distractions of the world and the divisions of thy

Church, and be pleased to stretch forth thy healing hand. Draw all men unto thee and one to another by the bands of thy love; make thy Church one, and fill it with thy Spirit, that by thy power it may unite the world in a sacred brotherhood of nations, wherein justice and mercy, faith, truth, and freedom may flourish, and thou mayest ever be glorified.

O THOU who art the light of the world, the desire of all nations, and the shepherd of our souls: let thy light shine in the darkness, and by the lifting up of thy Cross gather the peoples unto thee, that all the ends of the earth may see the salvation of God.

REMEMBER, O God, those multitudes who, though created in thine image, are ignorant of thy love: and grant that by our prayers and labours they may be delivered from all superstition and unbelief and brought to worship thee; through him whom thou hast sent to be our salvation, thy Son Jesus Christ our Lord.

O GOD, the Father of all mankind: we beseech thee to inspire us with such love, truth, and equity, that in all our dealings one with another we may shew forth our brotherhood in thee.

O GOD of unchangeable power and eternal light, look favourably on thy whole Church, that wonderful and sacred mystery: and, by the tranquil operation of thy perpetual providence, carry out the work of man's salvation. And let the whole world feel and see that things which were cast down are being raised up, that those which had grown old are being made new, and that all things are returning to perfection through him from whom they took their origin; even through our Lord Jesus Christ.

O LORD Jesus Christ, who on the Cross didst remember thy Mother and thy friend, make our homes to be homes of love. Spread thy grace over every relationship of human life, so that all our earthly love may be gathered up into the love of God, and thy Kingdom made manifest to men in the homes of thy people.

THE Lord make you to increase and abound in love one toward another, and toward all men; to the end he may stablish your hearts unblamable in holiness before our God and Father, at the coming of our Lord Jesus with all his saints. *Amen.*

HYMNS

A. & M.	S.P.	
218	170	God of mercy, God of grace
	320	Lord, while for all mankind we pray
	308	O God of earth and altar
	666	There's a wideness in God's mercy
	691	We thank thee, Lord, for this fair earth
268	702	Ye servants of the Lord
M.P. 89, 15–18		O greatly bless'd the people are

XXIV

CHRIST SHALL BE ALL IN ALL

*Till we all attain unto the unity of the faith, and of the know-
ledge of the Son of God, unto a fullgrown man, unto the measure
of the stature of the fulness of Christ.*

FOR this cause we bow our knees unto the Father of our
Lord Jesus Christ, from whom every family in heaven
and on earth is named:

That he would grant us, according to the riches of his
glory, that we may be strengthened with power through
his Spirit in the inward man;

That Christ may dwell in our hearts through faith; to the
end that we, being rooted and grounded in love, may be
strong to apprehend with all the saints what is the
breadth and length and height and depth;

And to know the love of Christ which passes knowledge, that we may be filled with all the fulness of God.

ALMIGHTY God, the inspirer of prophets and apostles, and
of every true and good thought and feeling in men: we
thank thee for the gift of thy Spirit, by which thou hast
enabled some in all ages to be the teachers and leaders of
their brethren; and we pray thee so to pour out the same
Spirit on us that we may know and understand the deep
things of God, and that love and goodness and all the
fruits of righteousness may abound in our lives, to thy
praise and glory.

O GOD of sure mercies, strengthen the weak hands,
confirm the feeble knees: let the eyes of the blind
be opened, and the ears of the deaf be unstopped. Let

waters of life break out in the wilderness, and streams in the desert. Cast up an highway for us, even the way of holiness, that the ransomed of the Lord may return and come to Zion, with songs of gladness and everlasting joy.

OUR FATHER . . .

PSALM

100. O be joyful in the Lord, all ye lands

48. Great is the Lord, and highly to be praised

LET us commend to God those for whom it is our special duty to pray: our parents and children; our brothers and sisters; our friends; all who have helped us by their prayers, advice, and example, by their sympathy and encouragement; our companions in work, society, and recreation; the unfriendly, the uncongenial, and any whom we dislike and find trying or difficult. Behold, how good and joyful a thing it is, brethren, to dwell together in unity!

MAY thy mercy and blessing, O Father of all, rest upon our land and nation: upon all the powers which thou hast ordained over us; our King, and all in authority under him; the ministers of State, the great councils of the nation, and all judges and magistrates; that we may lead a quiet and peaceable life in all godliness and honesty. Rule the hearts of men in all classes of our people, and draw all together in true brotherhood and sympathy; through Jesus Christ our Lord.

O ETERNAL Lord God, who alone spreadest out the heavens, and rulest the raging of the sea: be pleased to receive into thy protection all those who go down to the sea in ships and occupy their business in great waters; the guardians of our shores, and all who are in lightships and lighthouses. Preserve them both in body and soul; prosper their labours with good success, and in all time of danger be their defence; through Jesus Christ our Lord.

ALMIGHTY God, father of all mercies and giver of all comfort: deal graciously, we pray thee, with those who mourn; that, casting every care on thee, they may know the consolation of thy love; through Jesus Christ our Lord.

O GOD our Father, we humbly beseech thee to bless thy Church, and fill it with truth and grace. Where it is corrupt, purge it; where it is in error, direct it; where anything is amiss, reform it; where it is right, strengthen and confirm it; where it is wanting, furnish it; where it is rent asunder, heal its divisions, O thou holy one of Israel.

O LORD who, though thou wast rich, yet for our sake didst become poor, and hast taught us that whatever is done unto the least of thy brethren is done unto thee: give us grace always to be willing and ready to minister, as thou enablest us, to the necessities of our fellow creatures, and to extend the blessings of thy Kingdom over all the world; to thy praise and glory, who art God over all, blessed for ever.

O LORD Jesus, master of our lives: help us to glorify thee at all times in the thoughts of our minds, in the desires of our hearts, in the words of our lips, in the works of our hands, in the ways of our feet; as becomes those who are striving to follow thee.

Almighty God, give us grace that we may cast away the works of darkness, and put upon us the armour of light, now in the time of this mortal life, in which thy Son Jesus Christ came to visit us in great humility: that in the last day, when he shall come again in his glorious majesty to judge both the quick and the dead, we may rise to the life immortal; through him who liveth and reigneth with thee and the Holy Ghost, now and ever.

Unto him that sitteth on the throne, and unto the Lamb, be the blessing, and the honour, and the glory, and the dominion, for ever and ever. *Amen.*

HYMNS

A. & M.	S.P.	
300	440	All hail the power of Jesus' name
516		Before Jehovah's awful throne
299	472	Come, let us join our cheerful songs
219	87	Hail to the Lord's anointed
178	547	Jesu, the very thought of thee
	M.P. 93	The Lord doth reign, and cloth'd is he

XXV

I WILL COME TO YOU

As many as are led by the Spirit of God, these are sons of God.

The Spirit himself beareth witness with our spirit, that we are children of God.

O HOLY Spirit of life, who fillest all the world, we worship and adore thee. Spirit of light, who teachest all truth, we worship and adore thee. Source of all gifts of nature and of grace, of knowledge natural and super-natural, we worship and adore thee. For that thou hast made and endowed us, taught and reproved us, borne with us, recovered us, restored us; Lord and lifegiver, we worship and adore thee.

O GOD our Father, we lift up our hearts to thee this day in thankfulness: we humbly acknowledge thy mercy and thy truth, thy large and tender providence, thy nearness to us at all times, thy spirit of wisdom and might and peace, and the promises that lay hold of the things to come. God of all grace, Father of our Lord and Saviour, creator of our dying bodies, life and light of our undying souls, thy gifts are new every morning. May thy great love redeem us; and from the light of a true life below may we pass at length into that presence where there is fulness of joy, and abundance of peace, for ever; through the merits of Jesus Christ our Lord.

OUR FATHER . . .

H

PSALM

139, I–II. O Lord, thou hast searched me out, and known me

15. Lord, who shall dwell in thy tabernacle?

GOD, who dost teach the hearts of thy faithful people by sending to them the light of thy Holy Spirit: grant us by the same Spirit to have a right judgment in all things, and evermore to rejoice in his holy comfort; through the merits of Christ Jesus our Saviour, who liveth and reigneth with thee in the unity of the same Spirit, one God, world without end.

WE beseech thee to hear us, O God, that thy Spirit may lead us into all truth, revealing and interpreting to us the things of Christ:

That thy Spirit may enable us to walk in the way of Christ, and to offer him faithful and acceptable service:

That thou wilt make our lives rich in the fruits of the Spirit; love, joy, peace, longsuffering, kindness, goodness, faithfulness, gentleness, self-control:

That we may be led into that freedom which Christ gives to those who try to follow him; and that we may be enabled to keep the unity of the Spirit in the bond of peace.

O LOVING Father, we remember before thee all those who travel or whose work calls them to the distant places of the earth: in danger may they be given courage and endurance; in loneliness may they be helped by the knowledge that others are remembering them; in time of temptation may they have strength to hold fast to what they know to be right; and may the sense of thy presence and the knowledge of thy fatherly love ever be with them; we ask this for the sake of Jesus Christ our Lord.

ALMIGHTY Father, who by thy Son Jesus Christ hast sanctified labour to the welfare of mankind: prosper, we pray thee, the industries of this land, and all who are engaged therein; that, being shielded in their hardships and dangers, and receiving their due reward, they may praise thee by living according to thy will; through Jesus Christ our Lord.

QUICKEN, O God, the spirit of service throughout our country: help us to promote the common good, and to establish justice and fair-dealing for all men.

O GOD the Holy Spirit, who knowest how amid the burdens and anxieties of our daily life we so easily forget thee: inspire us with a continual sense of thy presence; teach us to hear and to heed thy voice; that we may be filled with thy grace now and evermore.

BLESSED Spirit of God, still with the tranquil inspiration of thy grace our restless souls, and give us peace: may we have faith to wait patiently upon the will of God and tarry the leisure of the Lord, that he may comfort our hearts and stablish us in his strength; through the might of thy holy indwelling.

O GOD, the strength of all them that put their trust in thee, mercifully accept our prayers: and, because through the weakness of our mortal nature we can do no good thing without thee, grant us the help of thy grace, that in keeping of thy commandments we may please thee both in will and deed; through Jesus Christ our Lord.

O LORD, who hast called us to be thy witnesses: have mercy upon us, who have known thy will but have failed to do our part. Cleanse us from unbelief and sloth, and fill us with hope and zeal; that we may do thy work, and bear thy Cross, and bide thy time, and see thy glory; who livest and reignest with the Father and the Holy Spirit, one God, world without end.

LOOK graciously upon us, O Holy Spirit: and give us, for our hallowing, thoughts that pass into prayer, prayers that pass into love, and love that passes into life with thee for ever.

GRACE, mercy, peace shall be with us, from God the Father, and from Jesus Christ, the Son of the Father, in truth and love. *Amen.*

HYMNS

A. & M.	S.P.	
670	177	Come down, O Love divine
673		Come, Holy Spirit, come
156		Come, thou Holy Spirit, come
672	520	Holy Spirit, truth divine
208		O Holy Spirit, Lord of grace
207	182	Our blest Redeemer, ere he breathed

XXVI

WALK IN THE LIGHT

If we walk in the light, as he is in the light, we have fellowship one with another, and the blood of Jesus his Son cleanseth us from all sin.

O JOYFUL light of the holy glory of the everlasting Father, which is in heaven, holy and blessed, Jesus Christ our Lord: at eventide and in the morning we have seen light; therefore we give thanks and praise to the Father, and to the Son, and to the Holy Spirit of God. Worthy art thou at all times to be praised with holy voices, Son of God, giver of life: therefore doth the world glorify thee.

W E thank thee, O God, for the work of thy Spirit within and beyond the bounds of thy visible Church. For his work in the world before the coming of Christ; through peaceful advance, through pain and tumult and war; especially in the history of our own country, through its heroes and leaders, in statecraft, law, and industry:

For the work of thy Spirit in science and commerce, in literature and art; and in the desire for true brotherhood between men of every class and nation:

For the work of thy Spirit in the Church, impelling us to spread the gospel throughout the whole world:

Glory be to thee, O Lord.

OUR FATHER . . .

PSALM

61. Hear my crying, O God

119, 89–96. O Lord, thy word

O GOD, by whom the meek are guided in judgment, and light rises up in darkness for the godly: grant to the rulers of the world, in all their doubts and uncertainties, the grace to ask what thou wouldst have them to do. May we be mindful of our duty to uphold them by our constant prayers; that the spirit of wisdom may save them from all false choices; that in thy light they may see light, and in thy straight path may not stumble; through Jesus Christ our Lord.

A LMIGHTY and most merciful God, who hast given the Bible to be the revelation of thy great love to man, and of thy power and will to save him: grant that our study of it may not be made in vain by the callousness or carelessness of our hearts; but that by it we may be confirmed in penitence, lifted to hope, made strong in service, and above all filled with the true knowledge of thee and of thy Son Jesus Christ.

O EVERLASTING God, who by thy Holy Spirit dost lead men to the knowledge of the truth: inspire, we pray thee, all who teach and all who learn; that they may have zeal to seek the truth, right judgment to discern it, wisdom to understand it, resolution to hold it fast, and faith to act upon it. Guide them in doubt and perplexity; deliver them from carelessness or irreverence, lest the word be heard and not heeded, believed and not obeyed, known and not loved; that all men may know thee the only true

God, and him whom thou didst send, even Jesus Christ our Lord.

O GOD, who by thy Spirit in our hearts dost lead men to desire thy perfection, to seek for truth, and to rejoice in beauty: illuminate and inspire, we beseech thee, all thinkers and writers, all artists and craftsmen; direct all teachers and students in the schools and colleges of our land; that in whatsoever is true and pure and lovely thy name may be hallowed, and thy Kingdom may come on earth.

FOR those who are in doubt and difficulty, sorrow and anguish of spirit, fear, ignorance, and blindness of heart: and for all who wish to believe in thee but cannot find thee; O Lord, let there be light.

ALMIGHTY God, who hast sent thy Spirit of truth to guide us into all truth: so rule our lives by thy power that we may be truthful in word, and deed, and thought. Keep us under thy gracious protection, that no fear or hope may ever make us false in act or speech. Cast out from us whatever loves or makes a lie, and bring us all into the perfect freedom of thy truth; through Jesus Christ thy Son our Lord.

O LORD, we need thee to teach us day by day, according to each day's opportunities and needs. Purify, we pray thee, our consciences. Our ears are dull, so that we cannot hear thy voice. Our eyes are dim, so that we cannot see thy tokens. Thou alone canst quicken our hearing, and purge our sight, and renew our hearts. Teach us to sit at thy feet, and to hear thy word.

GRANT to us, O God, this day to do whatever duty lies before us with cheerfulness and sincerity of heart. Help us in all things fearlessly to do what we know to be right. Save us from hypocrisy and pretence. Make us truthful, unselfish, and strong. And so bring us to the ending of the day unashamed and with a quiet mind.

MAY the Spirit, O God, who proceeds from thee, illuminate our minds and, as thy Son has promised, lead us into all truth; through our Lord Jesus Christ.

THE grace of our Lord Jesus Christ be with you all. *Amen.*

HYMNS

A. & M.	S.P.	
243	570	Lord, thy Word abideth
513	597	O God of truth, whose living word
698	256	O thou who camest from above
155	184	Spirit of mercy, truth, and love
360	303	Thou whose almighty Word
M.P.	121	I to the hills will lift mine eyes

XXVII

MORE THAN CONQUERORS

They that wait upon the Lord shall renew their strength; they shall mount up with wings as eagles; they shall run, and not be weary; they shall walk, and not faint.

Honour and power eternal be to thee, O God: King of kings and Lord of lords, who alone hast immortality, dwelling in light unapproachable, whom no man has seen, nor can see; and to thine only-begotten Son, who for us men and for our salvation came down from heaven, and was made man, and through his death and resurrection brought us life and immortality. Faithful is the saying: If we died with him, we shall also live with him.

Almighty God, in whom is no darkness, give to us thy light, that we may walk therein. Grant to us that where we cannot see we may be content to trust; that in all our ways, being guided and guarded by thee, we may be kept from falling, and pass at last through the gate of death into eternal life; through thy mercy in Jesus Christ our Lord.

OUR FATHER . . .

PSALM

27, 1–9. The Lord is my light, and my salvation; whom then shall I fear?

46. God is our hope and strength

Most holy and most merciful God, the strength of the weak, the rest of the weary, the comfort of the sorrowful, the Saviour of the sinful, and the refuge of thy children in every time of need: hear us, who ask for thy help.

When our faith is growing weak, and our love cold; when we are losing our vision of thee, and the spiritual world is not real to us:

When we are tempted to mean and wicked ways, and sin grows less sinful in our sight; when duty is difficult, and work is hard, and our burdens are heavy:

When the unknown future troubles us, and in our fears and anxieties we forget thine eternal love and mercy; when the last darkness shall close around us, and heart and flesh fail, and vain is the help of man:

Holy Father, help us.

REMEMBER, O gracious Father, for good the needs of all thy children: fill our garners with all manner of store; preserve our marriages in peace and concord; nourish our infants, lead forward our youth, sustain the aged, comfort the weak-hearted; gather together the scattered, restore the wanderers, and knit us all in the bonds of thy love.

O LORD Jesus Christ, who at thy first coming didst send thy messenger to prepare thy way before thee: grant that the ministers and stewards of thy mysteries may likewise so prepare and make ready thy way, by turning the hearts of the disobedient to the wisdom of the just; that, at thy second coming to judge the world, we may be found an acceptable people in thy sight, who livest and reignest with the Father and the Holy Spirit, ever one God, world without end.

ALMIGHTY God, grant that we may awake to the joy of this day: finding gladness in its toils and difficulties, in its pleasures and successes, in its failures and sorrows. Teach us to look always away from ourselves, beholding thy glory and the needs of the world. Give us the will and the strength to bring gladness to others, that with them we may stand to bear the burden and heat of the day, and offer to thee the praise of work well done; through Jesus Christ our Lord.

O HEAVENLY Father, the father of all wisdom, understanding, and true strength: we beseech thee to look mercifully upon us, and send thy Holy Spirit into our hearts; that we may be strengthened by the defence of thy right hand, and may manfully stand in the confession of thy faith and truth, and continue in the same unto our lives' end.

LORD and King, we pray thee this day for courage to face unpopularity for the sake of truth: to declare boldly our convictions, though they make us despised; to break with evil custom and opinions, though we are shunned and outcast. Give us strong hearts that will not fear what man may do unto us. Give us the spirit of boldness, that we may trample on any fear of our fellows, being strong in thee, and of a good courage.

O GOD, who knowest us to be set in the midst of so many and great dangers that, by reason of the frailty of our nature, we cannot always stand upright: grant to us such strength and protection as may support us in all dangers, and carry us through all temptations; through Jesus Christ our Lord.

Give unto us, O God, the spirit of brightness, that no shadow may oppress our spirits, and no gloom may darken the light by which others live: and that we may face with courage whatever the day may bring; for the sake of Jesus Christ our Lord.

Teach us, good Lord, to serve thee as thou deservest: to give, and not to count the cost; to fight, and not to heed the wounds; to toil, and not to seek for rest; to labour, and to ask for no reward save the joy of knowing that we do thy will.

Go forth into the world in peace: be of good courage; hold fast that which is good; render to no man evil for evil; strengthen the faint-hearted; support the weak; help the afflicted; honour all men; love and serve the Lord, rejoicing in the power of the Holy Spirit. And the blessing of God Almighty, Father, Son, and Holy Spirit, be upon you and remain with you for ever. *Amen.*

HYMNS

A. & M.	S.P.	
682	451	Awake, our souls! Away, our fears!
540	491	Fight the good fight with all thy might
	515	He who would valiant be
291	619	Oft in danger, oft in woe
270		Soldiers of Christ, arise
588	642	Soldiers of the Cross, arise!

XXVIII

BE YE HOLY

Worship the Lord in the beauty of holiness.
Blessed are the pure in heart: for they shall see God.

GREAT and marvellous are thy works, Lord God almighty: just and true are thy ways, thou King of saints. Who shall not fear thee, O Lord, and glorify thy name? For thou only art holy. All the nations shall come and worship before thee, for thy judgments are made manifest. Praise our God, all ye his servants, and ye that fear him, both small and great. Alleluia, for the Lord God omnipotent reigneth; let us be glad and rejoice, and give honour to his name.

WE come unto thee, O God our Father, with hearts troubled by the memory and the burden of our offences: of that which we ought to have done, but have not done; of that which we ought to have spoken, but have not spoken. Of these things, and of all our sins remembered and forgotten, we repent and turn to thee. Graciously forgive us; purify and strengthen our hearts; that we may walk steadfastly and uprightly before thee all our days, in the love and service of Jesus Christ our Lord.

FILL our mouths with thy praise, O Lord, and our lips with thanksgiving: that we may celebrate thy glory and majesty all the day long.

OUR FATHER . . .

PSALM

36, 1–9.   My heart sheweth me the wickedness of the ungodly

BENEDICTUS.   Blessed be the Lord God of Israel

M OST gracious God, we humbly beseech thee, as for this kingdom in general, so especially for the High Court of Parliament, [under our Sovereign Lord the King at this time assembled]: that thou wouldest be pleased to direct and prosper all their consultations to the advancement of thy glory, the good of thy Church, the safety, honour, and welfare of our Sovereign, and his dominions; that all things may be so ordered and settled by their endeavours, upon the best and surest foundations, that peace and happiness, truth and justice, religion and piety, may be established among us for all generations. These and all other necessaries, for them, for us, and thy whole Church, we humbly beg in the name and mediation of Jesus Christ, our most blessed Lord and Saviour.

O GOD, who willest not that any should live without comfort or die without hope: have compassion on the multitudes in our great cities who are crowded in wretched homes or oppressed by bitter poverty. Bless and inspire those who are working for their relief. Watch over the children, the sick, the aged. Rouse the careless, instruct the ignorant, recover the fallen. Stir the conscience of the whole nation, O Lord, and break the bonds of covetousness. Make plain the way of deliverance, and hasten the time when sin and shame shall be put away from among us; for the sake of Jesus Christ our Saviour.

LORD Jesus Christ, who hast sanctified all conflict for the truth: grant us, when we strive with one another, not to forget of what spirit we would be. Drive far from us the evil powers of distrust, suspicion, and contempt. When we differ, let us not condemn. Make us patient in argument, generous in judgment, slow to wrath. As thou givest us to see the right, make us strong to maintain it, yet always to be seekers of thy peace.

O GOD, whose blessed Son was manifested that he might destroy the works of the devil, and make us the sons of God, and heirs of eternal life: grant us, we beseech thee, that having this hope we may purify ourselves, even as he is pure; that, when he shall appear again with power and great glory, we may be made like unto him in his eternal and glorious Kingdom; where with thee, O Father, and thee, O Holy Ghost, he liveth and reigneth, ever one God, world without end.

O ETERNAL God, who hast taught us by thy holy Word that our bodies are temples of thy Spirit: keep us, we most humbly beseech thee, temperate and holy in thought, word, and deed; that with all the pure in heart we may see thee, and be made like unto thee in thy heavenly Kingdom; through Christ our Lord.

MOST merciful Lord, who hast taught us that the pure in heart shall see God: cleanse our hearts from all impurity; give us such hatred of evil and such love of all that is beautiful and strong, that we may be delivered from temptation and become a strength to others who are tempted.

O FATHER, light up the small duties of this day's life: may they shine with the beauty of thy face. May we believe that glory can dwell in the commonest task. We ask this in the name of Jesus Christ our Lord.

O SPIRIT of God, sanctify us wholly: that in spirit, soul, and body we may become thy temple. Dwell within us and be our God, and we will be thy servants.

GOD the Father, God the Son, and God the Holy Ghost, bless, preserve, and keep you: the Lord mercifully with his favour look upon you; and so fill you with all spiritual benediction and grace, that ye may so live in this life, that in the world to come ye may have life everlasting. *Amen.*

HYMNS

A. & M.	S.P.	
261	455	Blest are the pure in heart
671	458	Breathe on me, breath of God
	111	My spirit longs for thee
1		Now that the daylight fills the sky
163		Three in One, and One in Three
438	207	How bright these glorious spirits shine!
	Par. 66	

XXIX

THAT THEY MAY BE ONE

That they may all be one; even as thou, Father, art in me, and I in thee, that they also may be in us: that the world may believe that thou didst send me.

O GOD, who art and wast and art to come, the Father of the generations of men: we thank thee for all who have walked humbly with thee, especially those near and dear to us, in whom we have seen the vision of thy beauty. May we know that in the body and out of the body they are with thee. Make us glad in their living, and comfort and teach us through their dying. Unite us still, God of our souls, in one household of faith and love, one family in heaven and upon earth, in Jesus Christ our Lord.

O HEAVENLY Father: we thank thee for those who, out of the bitter memories of strife and loss, are seeking a more excellent way for the nations of the world, whereby justice and order may be maintained and the differences of peoples be resolved in equity. We pray thee to establish their purpose on sure foundations and to prosper their labours, that thy will may be done; for the sake of Jesus Christ our Lord.

OUR FATHER . . .

PSALM

84. O how amiable are thy dwellings

122. I was glad when they said unto me

I

MAY thy Holy Spirit, O God, guide all those who are bearing the burden of great responsibilities, (*especially....*): prosper their efforts for the welfare of the world. Inspire them with wise judgment, that they may help to build a brotherhood of mankind in the fatherhood of God. And may we all be set free from the spirit which leads to strife, from the temper which refuses to forgive, and has no wish to forget; and from lack of faith in thy power to change men's hearts. *O Lord hear our prayer*

BEHOLD, O God, our strivings after a truer and more abiding order. Give us visions which bring back a lost glory to the earth, and dreams which foreshadow that better order which thou hast prepared for us. Scatter every excuse of frailty and unworthiness; consecrate us all with a heavenly mission; and give us grace, according to our day, gladly to welcome and gratefully to fulfil it; through Jesus Christ our Lord.

HAVE mercy, O God, on the homeless, the unemployed, the bereaved, and the sorrowful, and give them comfort: on those who have none to pray for them, and none to succour them; on all who have brought punishment and trouble on themselves and those dear to them. Give them this day some token of grace, and some sign of hope; through Jesus Christ our Lord.

O HEAVENLY Father, who hast bestowed upon us the comfort of earthly friends: look in love upon those dear to us from whom we are separated. Protect them and keep them from all harm; prosper and bless them in all good things; suffer them never to be desolate or afraid, and let no shadow come between them and us to divide our hearts; but in thine own good time may we renew the fellowship of sight and hand; through Jesus Christ our Lord.

ALMIGHTY God, who dost ever look in fatherly love upon all who suffer: we ask thee to hear our prayers for all sick persons. Grant to each of them thy help in spirit and body, according to their need; cheer them and, if it be thy will, restore them; through Jesus Christ our Lord.

WE commend to thee, almighty God, the whole Christian Church throughout the world. Bless all in every place who call on the name of our Lord Jesus Christ. May the grace and power of the Holy Spirit fill every member, so that all the company of thy faithful people may bear witness for thee on the earth. Look in mercy on the errors and confusions of our time, and draw the hearts of believers nearer to the Lord Jesus Christ. If it be good in thy sight, heal the outward divisions of thy people, disposing the wills of all to a true union of order in the truth, for the work of the one Lord. And above all we pray for the unity of the Spirit, through whom alone we are guided into all truth. *O Lord hear our prayer.*

O LORD Jesus Christ, who didst pray for thy disciples *OVER* that they might be one, even as thou art one with the Father: draw us to thyself, that in common love and obedience to thee we may be united to one another in the fellowship of the one Spirit, and the world may believe that thou art Lord, to the glory of God the Father.

O GOD, who hast built thy Church upon the foundation of the apostles and prophets, Jesus Christ himself being the head corner-stone: grant us so to be joined
together in unity of spirit by their doctrine, that we may
be made an holy temple acceptable unto thee; through
Jesus Christ our Lord.

VOUCHSAFE, we beseech thee, almighty God, to the
whole Christian people unity, peace, and true concord, both visible and invisible; through Jesus Christ our
Lord.

THE God of patience and of comfort grant you to be
of the same mind one with another according to
Christ Jesus: that with one accord ye may with one mouth
glorify the God and Father of our Lord Jesus Christ.
Amen.

HYMNS

A. & M.	S.P.	
	485	Eternal ruler of the ceaseless round
595		Holy Father, in thy mercy
221	557	Let saints on earth in concert sing
215	249	The Church's one foundation
274	678	Through the night of doubt and sorrow
604		Thy hand, O God, has guided
M.P. 122, 6–9		Pray that Jerusalem may have

XXX

ROOTED AND GROUNDED IN LOVE

Beloved, let us love one another: for love is of God; and every one that loveth is begotten of God, and knoweth God. He that loveth not knoweth not God; for God is love.

Beloved, if God so loved us, we also ought to love one another.

LET us give praise and thanks to our Lord God: God who made all things by the word of his power, King and ruler of the world, glorious in beauty and truth and love.

O PRAISE the Lord, for it is a good thing to sing praises unto our God: yea, a joyful and pleasant thing it is to be thankful. He healeth those that are broken in heart: and giveth medicine to heal their sickness. Great is our Lord, and great is his power: yea, and his wisdom is infinite.

ALMIGHTY God, Father of all mercies: we thine unworthy servants do give thee most humble and hearty thanks for all thy goodness and loving-kindness to us, and to all men. We bless thee for our creation, preservation, and all the blessings of this life; but, above all, for thine inestimable love in the redemption of the world by our Lord Jesus Christ, for the means of grace and for the hope of glory. And, we beseech thee, give us that due sense of all thy mercies, that our hearts may be unfeignedly thankful, and that we shew forth thy praise, not only with our lips, but in our lives; by giving up ourselves to thy service, and by walking before thee in holiness and righteousness all our days; through Jesus

Christ our Lord, to whom with thee and the Holy Ghost be all honour and glory, world without end.

OUR FATHER . . .

PSALM

85. Lord, thou art become gracious unto thy land

138. I will give thanks unto thee, O Lord, with my whole heart

O GOD our Father, we have sinned against thee and against our fellow men in thought, in word, and in deed; we have not loved thee with all our heart; we have not loved our neighbours as ourselves. Have mercy upon us, we humbly beseech thee; cleanse us from our sins, and help us to overcome our faults; through Jesus Christ our Lord.

GOD our Father, shew forth thy loving-kindness, we pray thee, to any who are or feel themselves neglected, and who are little loved, or forgotten. Comfort all who mourn for the loss of those dear to them; be with them in their sorrow; give them faith to look beyond the troubles of this present time, and to know that neither life nor death can separate them from thy love, which is in Christ Jesus our Lord.

O GOD, who art everywhere present, look down with thy mercy upon those who are absent from among us. Keep them safe in body, soul, and spirit, that they may be presented faultless before the presence of thy glory with exceeding joy; through Jesus Christ our Lord.

GRANT us, O Lord, to love thee with all our heart, with all our mind, and with all our soul, and our neighbour for thy sake: that the grace of brotherly love may dwell in us, and all envy, harshness, and ill will may die in us. May we rejoice in the happiness and good success of others, sympathize with them in their sorrows, and put away all harsh judgments and envious thoughts; and so follow thee, who thyself art true and perfect love.

O MOST loving Father, who hast taught us to give thanks for all things, to dread nothing but the loss of thee, and to cast all our cares on thee who carest for us: preserve us from faithless fears and worldly anxieties, that no clouds of this mortal life may hide from us the light of that love which is immortal, and which thou hast shewn to us in thy Son Jesus Christ our Lord.

VOUCHSAFE, we beseech thee, O God, to strengthen and confirm all thy faithful people: and to lift them up more and more continually to heavenly desires.

O GOD, the unfailing strength of all who trust in thee, grant us in our duties thy help: in perplexity thy guidance, in danger thy protection, and in sorrow thy peace. Keep us, by thy continual grace, on the narrow way that leads to life; and, when our day of pilgrimage is over and we pass through the night of death, be thou, O Lord God, our everlasting light; through Jesus Christ our Saviour.

O CHRIST our Saviour, give us grace to desire thee with our whole heart: that so desiring we may seek and find thee, and so finding thee we may love thee, and loving thee we may hate those sins from which thou hast redeemed us, by the power of thine eternal sacrifice.

O LORD, who in the hour of death didst commend thy spirit into the loving hands of thy heavenly Father: grant that we may not fear to look forward to the hour of our own departure, knowing that through the grave and gate of death we shall pass with thee to our joyful resurrection, who livest and reignest, God for evermore.

THE Lord direct your hearts into the love of God, and into the patience of Christ. *Amen.*

HYMNS

A. & M.	S.P.	
703		Beloved, let us love: love is of God
	408	From all that dwell below the skies
210	507	Gracious Spirit, Holy Ghost
190	549	Jesus, thou joy of loving hearts
551		May the grace of God our Saviour
379	350	Now thank we all our God

INDEX TO PRAYERS

[The page-numbers may refer either to words or subjects]

WORSHIP, or PRAISE, or THANKSGIVING, will be found at the opening of each service.

INDEX OF PSALMS

HYMNS, METRICAL PSALMS, AND PARAPHRASES
Index of First Lines

K

ACKNOWLEDGEMENTS

THANKS are due to the following for permission to reprint prayers in this book—the name of the publication from which prayers have been reproduced is given in brackets— Messrs. Philip Allan & Co. Ltd. ('A Guide to Prayer'); Messrs. Allenson & Co. Ltd. ('Great Souls at Prayer'); Messrs. J. M. Dent & Sons Ltd. and the Ven. Leslie Hunter ('Devotional Services for Public Worship'); Messrs. W. Heffer & Sons Ltd. and Mrs. N. C. Sherwood ('The Road'); Messrs. Hodder & Stoughton and Sir George Adam Smith; Messrs. Kegan Paul, Trench, Trubner & Co. Ltd. (a prayer by George Dawson from 'A Collection of Prayers'); Messrs. Longmans Green & Co. Ltd. ('Per Christum Vinces', 'A Book of Modern Prayers'); the same and the Rev. E. Milner White ('A Cambridge Bede Book'); the same and the Society of St. John the Evangelist ('An Intercessory Manual'); the same and Miss Diana Ponsonby and Miss L. H. M. Soulsby ('Lord, Teach us to Pray'); Messrs. Macmillan & Co. Ltd. and Mrs. Aitken ('Building the Walls'); the same and the Rev. Arthur Westcott (prayers by Bishop Westcott); Messrs. A. R. Mowbray & Co. Ltd. ('Sursum Corda'); Messrs. Rivington & Co. Ltd. (a prayer by Sir Arthur Hort from 'School Prayers for Weekday Mornings'); the Copyright Committee of the Central Board of Finance of the Church of England (the Prayer-book as proposed in 1928); the Student Christian Movement Press ('A Book of Prayers for Students', 'A Devotional Diary', 'Prayers New and Old', 'Everyday Prayers'); the S.P.C.K. ('A Book of Prayers for Everyman', 'Acts of Devotion', and prayers by Christina Rossetti); Messrs. William Smith & Son ('A Book of Simple Prayers'); Messrs. J. Whitaker & Sons Ltd. ('The Narrow Way'); the National Free Church Council ('Yet Another Day' by Dr. J. H. Jowett); the Uppingham Prayer-book; Lady Laura Ridding ('A Litany of Remembrance'); Miss Barton ('The Challenge'); Mrs. Percy Dearmer ('The

Sanctuary'); the Bishop of Croydon, on behalf of the Angli-
can Evangelical Group Movement ('The Splendour of God');
the Rev. Dr. Archibald Fleming; the Ven. Leslie Hunter
('The Kingdom, the Power, and the Glory'); the Rev. G. H.
Russell ('Intercession Services').

Thanks for much help and advice is also due to several
individuals, among whom should be especially mentioned
Sir Walford Davies, Canon Harold Anson, the Very Rev.
F. W. Dwelly, the Ven. Leslie Hunter, the Rev. H. L. Johnston,
the Rev. Hugh Martin, the Rev. W. Charter Piggott, Dr.
Montague Rendall, Canon R. O. P. Taylor, the Rev. T. B.
Stewart Thomson, the Society of the Sacred Mission at Kel-
ham, and members of the B.B.C. Central Religious Advisory
Committee. Some of the above have either written prayers
for the book or have permitted the use of their own prayers
already published. It should be understood that responsibility
for the book as a whole rests with the B.B.C. alone.

The utmost care has been taken in tracing sources of the
prayers here printed; but, in a book of several hundred prayers,
it is possible that the originals of one or two may have
escaped notice or have been found impossible to trace.
Should there be any such error, it will be remedied in subse-
quent editions.

This book is available bound in
the following styles:

PAPER   *Price* 1s., *by post* 1s. 3d.
CLOTH *Price* 1s. 6d.   1s. 9d.
LEATHER *Price* 5s.   5s. 3d.

PRINTED IN GREAT BRITAIN AT
THE UNIVERSITY PRESS, OXFORD
BY JOHN JOHNSON
PRINTER TO THE UNIVERSITY